LOST
TEXAS TREASURE

LOST
TEXAS TREASURE

Sunken Ships, Rawhide Maps and Buried Plunder

W. CRAIG GAINES

THE
History
PRESS

Published by The History Press
Charleston, SC
www.historypress.com

Front cover, bottom left: Many Spanish coins have been recovered from Padre Island. *National Park Service*.

First published 2022

ISBN 9781540252814

Library of Congress Control Number: 2022935422

Notice: The information in this book is true and complete to the best of our knowledge. It is offered without guarantee on the part of the author or The History Press. The author and The History Press disclaim all liability in connection with the use of this book.

CONTENTS

Introduction: Texas Treasure   7

1. Treasures by County   9
2. Spanish Treasure Ships   152
3. Lost Mines   154
4. Border Wars   157
5. Texas Independence and the Mexican-American War
        Treasure   160
6. Jesse James, Other Outlaws and Their Loot   162
7. Jean Lafitte and Pirates   164
8. Shipwrecks   166

Bibliography   169
Index   177
About the Author   191

CONTENTS

Introduction

TEXAS TREASURE

I am fascinated by the diversity of Texas history and its lost treasure, lost mines and shipwreck tales. Texas was part of Native American, Spanish, Mexican, Texan and American lands and has the legends and stories to prove it. I've lived in and traveled throughout Texas gathering information and experiences useful in writing this book. Most legends come from enhancements of actual historical events. I have added history and information to these legends to weave a story of lost Texas treasure.

During the Spanish colonial period, the Spanish Crown claimed all minerals on Spanish lands, so prospecting and recovering minerals could only be legally done with permits and approval from the Spanish king's agents. Much unreported prospecting and mining may have been done. Formal documentation is lacking for most lost mine stories. Early American explorers and prospectors encountered a number of old diggings and rumors of lost Indian, Spanish and Mexican mines. Some lost and abandoned mines likely had exhausted their easily recoverable minerals, but as technology and product prices increase, these mineral deposits could become economic to exploit.

Early legends and stories of lost mines and lost treasure took place when there were few towns, so their locations were pegged to mountains, rivers and streams. Stories like that of Chief Yellow Wolf's lost mine, which was "a three-day ride west," are vague. A three-day ride for a Comanche on a horse covered a lot of ground.

Newspapers published many lost treasure and lost mine stories, as readers were interested in lost wealth—and maybe finding some for themselves. Values and potential values of lost treasures in this book are based on what others have written. Often, these values were unreasonable. Writers J. Frank Dobie, Thomas Penfield, Robert Marx and Thomas P. Terry gathered many treasure trove stories in their books. As metal detecting became a hobby in the late 1960s, a number of magazines focused on treasure and the Old West published lost treasure and lost mine stories, which I have used. The discovery in 1965 and recovery of treasure in 1967 from a sunken 1554 Spanish fleet off Padre Island vastly increased interest in lost Texas treasure.

I have tried to briefly present each legend, story and history based on my research, analysis and understanding. Many lost treasures and lost mines have more extensive writeups in books and articles. Where a tale covers more than one county, I noted it, and I have included separate entries by county. Where possible, several stories or versions of stories have been consolidated. Some tales have been retold so many times that there are a number of different accounts and multiple locations. I attempted to sort through a lot of information and present it in a logical sequence. Errors of interpretation and information are likely. These stories are often based on oral traditions. Where stories have been proven to be fraudulent, I have stated so, based on my historical research. At times, the production of fake treasure maps was a cottage industry, so some tales likely involved fake maps leading to treasure that didn't exist.

Many areas with treasure lore are part of Texas state lands, federal lands or other protected lands, but much of Texas is in private ownership. The treasures you can easily find throughout Texas are its people, varied landscapes and history.

W. Craig Gaines
Tulsa, Oklahoma
2022

Chapter 1

TREASURES BY COUNTY

ANDREWS COUNTY

Shafter Lake Treasure

Army soldier William Rufus "Pecos Bill" Shafter won the Medal of Honor in the Civil War and was a brigadier general in the Spanish-American War. Shafter and a group of soldiers reportedly guarded two wagonloads of gold from Mexico. While being trailed by Comanches, Shafter's command took a shortcut over the playa now called Shafter Lake. The water was shallow in the almost dry lakebed, but the two wagons broke down in the middle of the lake. As the Comanches got closer, Shafter and his men supposedly abandoned the wagons and the gold. The Indians ransacked the two wagons and set them afire. Shafter and his men never returned for the gold. In 1901 and 1931, wagon parts were found in Shafter Lake, giving fuel to the story of the lost gold. Shafter Lake is in an oil field now.

ANGELINA COUNTY

Apple Springs Cache

See Trinity County.

Boone's Ferry Treasures

See Tyler County.

Cannon Treasure

Treasure was supposedly placed in a cannon and hidden on the Nueces River, not far from Diboll or northeast of Corrigan. It could be in Polk County.

Church Treasure

Prior to 1690, church treasure may have been cached near Lufkin, close to where three aligned old oak trees once stood.

Flower Hamilton Cache

See Sabine County.

Indian Gold Mine

See Tyler County.

ARANSAS COUNTY
Colonel Yell

See San Patricio County.

Lost Spanish Payroll

Near False Live Oak Point on St. Joseph Island's south end, at Aransas Pass, Indians reportedly attacked a Spanish mule train carrying treasure. The Spaniards buried their treasure before being killed. A Rockport man may have found this treasure. It could be in Refugio County and is similar to "False Live Oak Pirate Treasure"; *see* Calhoun County.

Philadelphia

The American steamship *Philadelphia* sank on March 1, 1868, in Aransas Pass with $10,000 in specie aboard. It could be in San Patricio County.

Pirate Chest

A pirate chest full of gold was supposedly hidden somewhere on St. Joseph Island. It could be in Calhoun County.

Vincent's Cathedral Treasure

Another cache said to have been buried on St. Joseph Island was church ornaments and treasure bound for a cathedral in Veracruz that a man named Vincent salvaged from a wreck. He buried it for safekeeping until the priest who had been on the wrecked vessel could return. Five years later, the priest returned. Vincent claimed he couldn't remember where he buried the treasure, as the land's surface had changed. The priest accused Vincent of stealing the church treasure. Outraged, Vincent murdered the priest. Vincent later drowned or committed suicide. Vincent originally came to St. Joseph Island in 1880 on a French ship, which was wrecked there. He built his home on the island with wood from that wreck. Hidden church ornaments and treasure may still be at Vincent's Point.

ARCHER COUNTY

Lake Wichita Nuggets

Gold nuggets were rumored to have been cached south of Lake Wichita, in a pothole. The wagon train massacre's lone survivor of an Indian attack hid in a pothole in a ravine. In the pothole he found gold nuggets. He covered the nuggets with dirt to hide them. The survivor reached civilization and tried to retrace his steps to find the nuggets but was unable to find them. Another gold nugget cache, or maybe the same one, was supposed to be near Wichita Falls. These could be California Gold Rush 49ers caches.

Robber's Cache

A robber's cache of gold and silver coins in saddlebags was said to be halfway between two big oak trees southeast of Archer City, near the West Fork of the Trinity River.

Armstrong County

Casner Treasure

See Randall County.

Atacosa County

Found Mexican Dollars

J. Frank Dobie's *Legends of Texas* volume 1 stated that some 800 Mexican dollars were found in Atacosa County under a mesquite tree.

Horse Trader's Cache

See Bexar County.

Saddlebags of Gold

A legend indicated two saddlebags full of gold were cached southeast of Pleasanton inside a hollow tree.

Bandera County

Mission San Saba Mines Treasure

During a Comanche, Tonkawa and Hasinai Indian attack on Mission Santa Cruz de San Saba in 1758, Spanish soldiers from San Saba Presidio (Presidio de San Luis de las Amarillas) were said to have escorted two pack trains, of about thirty-seven mules each, bound for San Antonio to escape. Each mule reportedly carried about three hundred pounds of mined silver from the San Saba mines. After a running battle with Indians, the Spanish mule trains were trapped at Olmos Pass. The Spaniards were surrounded near a spring, where they hid their silver in an opening in the sandstone hills. They covered the entrance with soil and rocks. The Indians supposedly killed around sixty Spaniards, but one old man was wounded and pretended to be dead. As he struggled to reach San Antonio, he met friendly Lipan Apaches. Dying, he drew a map of the treasure site and gave it to a young Indian girl to deliver to a San Antonio

San Saba Presidio was built to protect mines and settlers. Many lost mines and treasures are associated with this fort. *Author.*

priest. The map was never delivered to the priest. It was acquired by various people who looked unsuccessfully for the treasure. At least one or two silver bars have been recovered from the Olmos Pass area. This silver could be in Bell or Bexar County.

BEE COUNTY

Hide Hunters Treasure

In 1892, a hide hunter was rumored to have hidden $300 to $400 southeast of Beeville.

Lost Money

Some $40,000 in gold from a kidnapping was reportedly hidden near or south of Beeville. Another version has the money hidden by a Brownsville man near Beeville on his way to San Antonio. He camped near two oak trees on the west side of the road. When he saw riders heading his way, he buried his gold under his campfire and fled. The outlaws captured and tortured him to try to get him to disclose where his money was.

After being taken to Mexico, the Brownsville man escaped. When he recovered from his ordeal, he was unable to find where he had hidden his money.

Mexican Trader Cache

About seven miles southwest of Beeville and south of Aransas Creek, a Mexican trader supposedly hid $500 in gold and silver coins.

Nueces Flats Cache

A Mexican cache of $12,000 in gold was rumored hidden on a hill between Tigre Ranch and Coma Ranch in Nueces Flats, some five miles south of Olmos. Some believe this cache was recovered. It could be in Live Oak County or San Patricio County.

BELL COUNTY

Lost Gold

Near where three rivers joined to form the Little River, about sixty-five miles north of Austin and fifteen miles south of Temple, gold was reportedly buried in 1750 under a large tree marked by a brass spike.

Lost Stone Jar Treasure

A stone jar and iron chests containing treasure were said to have been hidden south of Salado.

Mission San Saba Mines Treasure

See Bandera County.

Spanish Salado Creek Treasure

Marquis de San Miguel de Aguayo and his explorers were rumored to have cached $20 million in Spanish gold bullion in a mine shaft. The Spanish were also said to have mined gold and silver on Salado Creek, which they hid in the mountains near Salado.

Many years later, an Indian called Pablo Juarez lived in a cave and reportedly had gold bars at times. Pablo Juarez told his friend Guerra that $36 million was in a cave. After Pablo Juarez's death, Guerra claimed he entered the cave through a riverbank opening. He saw a treasure room containing a gold bull with ruby eyes and piles of silver and gold bullion. He left the cave exhausted and ill. According to this tale, Guerra spent eight months in the hospital and never recovered any treasure. Extensive digging for this lost treasure has been done in an area about eighteen miles southwest of Belton, just south of Stillhouse Hollow Reservoir. Unsuccessful excavations occurred in 1928, 1938, and 1965.

Steinheimer's Millions

North of Temple, several million dollars' worth of gold and silver were said to have been hidden by Karl Steinheimer. Steinheimer was a German slave trader, pirate and adventurer who eventually owned a Mexican mine. Upon discovering his long-lost German sweetheart had moved to St. Louis, he cashed in his wealth. With two companions, he gathered ten mule loads of silver and gold and headed toward St. Louis about late 1838. Steinheimer started out with members of the Mexican army for protection. Upon hearing an armed Texas force was ahead, he left the Mexican soldiers and took a parallel route north, then hid his vast treasure. A copper stake or brass stake marked the cache, near where the Leon River and Lampasas River join. The stake was about forty feet above the ground in an old oak tree. The treasure was supposed to be forty to fifty feet from the tree. Steinheimer took only a few coins for his immediate needs before continuing his journey. Indians attacked and killed his men and critically injured Steinheimer with an arrow in his shoulder. A dying Steinheimer found some people who helped him. Before dying, Steinheimer wrote a letter with a map showing where he hid his treasure. The letter and map reached his sweetheart in St. Louis. Some members of his sweetheart's family came to Texas looking for the treasure but reportedly never found it. Another version of this story indicated that $5 million in gold dust and nuggets was hidden on a hill ten to seventy miles north of Austin, where three streams (Lampasas River, Salado Creek and Little River) intersect and form one river.

R.E. Shackelford found a bronze spike in 1967 and looked for the treasure but did not find it. L.D. Bertillion, who had heard the tale in his

Texas travels, wrote about it in *Legends of Texas* volume 1. J. Frank Dobie also wrote about this tale in *Coronado's Children*. Xanthus Carson wrote a comprehensive article in *Treasure* magazine on this cache. It could be in Travis County or Williamson County.

BEXAR COUNTY

Alamo Cave Treasure

This treasure cave was said to have been near San Antonio.

Alamo Treasure

A legend indicated that in the famous Alamo (Mission San Antonio de Valero), a large rock covered stairs leading down to a tunnel under the mission. The tunnel exited out near San Pedro Park and was for priests to escape if the mission was surrounded by enemies. It was claimed that a treasure was hidden in the tunnel, possibly during a 1781 Indian raid. Santa Anna's Mexican army killed almost two hundred Texas revolutionaries at the Alamo in 1836.

Horse Trader's Cache

About fifteen miles southwest of San Antonio, a horse trader was rumored to have hidden a wooden money box. It could be in Atascosa County or Medina County.

Mission San Saba Mines Treasure

See Bandera County.

Pancho Villa Treasures

A Pancho Villa loot site was said to be fifteen feet from an orange tree in the first church with high walls coming from the southwest into San Antonio. On her deathbed, in 1956, Delores Agilero Vasquez claimed Pancho Villa buried five treasures worth $1.5 million in the United States. Another tale of Pancho Villa loot near San Antonio includes $75,000 in gold coins

Above: The Alamo has a legend about lost treasure. *National Archives.*

Left: Famous bandit strongman Pancho Villa was said to have left behind a number of Texas treasures. *National Archives.*

hidden near the Presidio Crossing of the Nueces River. *See* Kleberg County, "Cinenia Caches/Pancho Villa Treasure"; Nueces County, "Pancho Villa Treasures"; and Starr County, "Pancho Villa Treasure."

Roundout Train Robbery Loot

On June 12, 1924, in Roundout, Illinois, the Newton Brothers Gang robbed a train of $2 million to $3 million in cash, jewelry and securities in mailbags— the largest train robbery haul up to that time. At least $100,000 in cash was never recovered, according to authorities. One account said Jess (Joseph) Newton hid about $35,000 in cash while he was drunk in San Antonio. Jess Newton claimed he buried it northwest of San Antonio. The next day, when he sobered up and decided to go to Mexico, he couldn't find it. Jess Newton was arrested and imprisoned for only about a year, since he helped the Texas Rangers and other law enforcement in the case. About $400,000 in loot was supposed to have been hidden near San Antonio, according to one tale. Maybe it was to the north of San Antonio, by one account, but another account claimed it was $350,000 hidden southeast of San Antonio. The entire Newton Gang was arrested and went to prison. The Newton Gang stole more money than any other notorious bank and train robbers.

Santiago's Treasure Cave

Treasure was supposedly cached near Seminole Hill in a cave.

Seminole Hill Treasure

Confederate guerrilla leader William C. Quantrill was rumored to have cached loot on Seminole Hill, just west of San Antonio. He and his guerrilla band were wintering in Texas after Union soldiers chased them out of Missouri.

Civil War Confederate guerrilla leader William C. Quantrill reportedly hid a cache near Seminole Hill near San Antonio. *Library of Congress.*

Swedish Emigrant Cache

Before the Civil War, a legend indicated Swedish emigrants' gold nuggets (or money) worth $20,000 were cached near Salado Creek. The treasure was intended to buy land. While the man who was in charge of the pooled treasure was away, four robbers, posing as landowners wanting to sell land, killed the man's wife and two daughters, stole the treasure and burned their cabin down. Before dying, the woman revealed who attacked her family. A posse tracked down and killed the murderers, but the treasure was missing. Everyone believed the robbers had hidden the treasure.

Trader's Gold

Near the Nueces River, below the Presidio Crossing, Indians supposedly attacked a trader. He reportedly hid $75,000 in gold coins on the top of a little hill near San Antonio.

BLANCO COUNTY

Spanish Pack Train Treasure

See Hays County.

BRAZORIA COUNTY

Augusta

The *Augusta* sank on June 4, 1846, at the mouth of the Brazos River while carrying $25,000 in specie.

Campbell's Bayou Treasure

Campbell's Bayou was named after one of Jean Lafitte's pirates, Jim Campbell. Campbell settled down on that branch of Chocolate Bayou, near Liverpool, after Jean Lafitte left Galveston Island. Campbell and another pirate, Captain Snyder, lived in a small house. They had money, so it was believed they had hidden pirate treasure. Campbell died, and Captain Snyder vanished. One tale had a mysterious vessel come to the area; then the locals claimed to have found a hole with the imprint of a chest and a broken jar with imprints of coins in the wax seal. *Legends of Texas* volume 2 has a good telling of this tale.

Colonel Rufus

Off Velasco on June 15, 1897, the *Colonel Rufus* sank with $1,000 in specie.

E.A. Ogden

The *E.A. Ogden* sank in 1850 at the mouth of the Brazos River with $40,000 in specie.

Holt's Treasure

A man named Holt supposedly hid money in a rose garden at Alvin. It could be in Galveston County.

Lively

See Galveston County.

Lost Safe

The 1875 hurricane destroyed the small town of Quintana, located a few miles south of Freeport. The five-foot-tall safe in the hotel there vanished when the storm demolished the hotel. The safe may have contained gold and silver coins and other treasure, as it was the only safe in the small town.

Pirate Ship Treasure

A legend claimed that, about 1816, a crew of pirates took their treasure (worth $10 million) off their ship and buried it near the mouth of the San Bernard River as a hurricane approached. The hurricane sank the pirate ship. The only survivor said he did not bury the treasure, but other crewmen did. He looked unsuccessfully for the treasure. Indians later told settlers they had seen ship wreckage at the mouth of the San Bernard River after a big storm. This story is from *Lost Legends of Texas* volume 2.

Yellowstone

At the Brazos River's mouth, the American sidewheel steamer *Yellowstone* sank in 1837 while transporting $40,000 in specie.

Brazos County

Boonville Treasure

Several treasures were supposed to be near the ghost town of Boonville.

Brewster County

Death Hill Treasure

This cache of gold coins was said to be near Emory Peak in Big Bend National Park.

Gaines Treasure

Gideon Gaines supposedly hid a can containing gold in the Chisos Mountains during an Indian attack. Before he was killed by the Indians, he wrote a message about the treasure location and put it in a tin can. About twenty-five years later, his skeleton was found with a message signed "Gideon Gaines" in a tin can. Some thought he died some distance from where he hid his treasure.

Gold Cairns Treasure

This cache was rumored to be in the Chisos Mountains in Big Bend National Park.

Gold Peak Lost Mine

A lost mine was said to have been near Terlingua, which was a silver-mining town with mines nearby.

A lost mine was said to be near the silver-mining ghost town of Terlingua. *Library of Congress.*

Humphrey Treasure

This treasure was supposed to be in the Boquillas area.

Lost Chisos Gold Mine/Lost Ranger Gold Mine/ Lost Phantom Mine

West of the Rio Grande, a Spanish mine was reportedly near the top of the Lost Mine Trail between Hot Springs and Vincente Canyon or between the Maravillas River (Creek) and San Francisco River. It may have been near Horse Mountain. The mountain where the mine was located had its peak shadow appear in the Mission San Vincente's doorway at a certain day and time. The mission and Presidio de San Vincente are in Mexico on the Rio Grande, about two miles upstream of San Vincente, and were established in 1773. The Spanish enslaved Indians to work in the mine. A lost mine may also be near the Rio Grande about eleven miles above Boquillas, Mexico, in Big Bend National Park. It was also claimed to be in the Chisos Mountains near Juniper Canyon. Likely this legend is about several lost mines, as there is a lot of confusion on locations.

Lost Mine Peak Mine and Treasure

A legend indicated a lost silver mine was near Lost Mine Peak in Big Bend National Park. It was said that a group of Spaniards hid twenty mule loads of silver bars at the bottom of a waterfall south of Lost Mine Peak before an Indian attack. A rockslide covered the area, and the Spaniards couldn't recover their gold. A rancher reportedly found a silver bar near the Old Smugglers Trail near Lost Mine Peak.

The Lost Chisos Gold Mine and other lost mines were said to be in the Chisos Mountains. *National Archives.*

Lost Silver Bars

Near Pine Canyon in Big Bend National Park, silver bullion was said to have been cached.

Luiz Terrazas Treasures

A legend indicated that during a Mexican revolution, Luiz Terrazas of Chihuahua, Mexico, cached $3 million in gold bullion and other treasure near the Rio Grande. It might be hidden at Rosillos Mountain. Everyone who knew the cache's location died before they could recover it.

Manuel Ortega Treasure

Before Mexican bandit Manuel Ortega was killed in 1817, he reportedly cached loot from about a dozen wagons somewhere near Black Rock Peak and Elephant Mountain, not far from Calamity Creek.

Mexican Bandits Loot

Mexican bandits may have hidden loot about two miles north of Boquillas near the Tornillo River.

Mexican Miners Treasure

When attacked, Mexican miners supposedly hid about three hundred pounds of gold about fifteen miles west of the Maravillas River (Creek). The surviving miners could not locate their cache.

The rugged mountains of the Big Bend National Park have many tales of lost treasure. *Library of Congress.*

Paisano Pass Gold

A road cut near Alpine (formerly Murphyville) supposedly contained gold flakes entombed in blue shale. In the 1880s, two men in a Southern Pacific Railroad construction crew found a gold deposit in the area and quit. They got enough gold to enable them to spend a lot of money in San Antonio. Another version was that a railroad engineer called Hughes took rock samples in the Paisano Pass area west of Alpine. He had them assayed in Denver, with one sample turning out to be gold. Hughes quit his railroad job and tried to find the black ledge that held the gold but never did.

Many years later, an Alpine art teacher collected clay at various locations to make pottery. In one road cut between Alpine and Marfa near the railroad, she found bluish clay and took some. When she later fired a pot out of it, the pot had impurities that came out on the surface. A sample showed the impurities to be gold. The art teacher couldn't find the location of the gold again, as she had sampled many locations.

Near Paisano Pass west of Alpine, Benito Ordones claimed to have discovered gold bullion stacked in a box canyon. The bullion was too heavy to carry, so he scraped off some gold as proof. He claimed it was Spanish gold but never seems to have gone back to retrieve it. In 1939, a man with a

Old mines and lost mines are in the Big Bend National Park. *Library of Congress.*

map to the gold bars got a party to search for them. Some landmarks were missing, so they did not find anything. This gold could be in Presidio County.

Sam Bass Brewster County Loot

Outlaw Sam Bass supposedly cached loot in a cave on Packsaddle Mountain. Another location of Sam Bass's loot was said to be Sue Peak, where $60,000 may have been hidden. Some stories claim this treasure was hidden by other outlaws.

Sanderson Loot

A treasure of $50,000 in gold or silver coins was reportedly hidden near San Vincente. This loot was from an 1891 Southern Pacific Railroad train robbery near Sanderson, Terrell County, by six outlaws. A detachment of Texas Rangers came across their camp. Three outlaws were captured (or killed) and their leader killed in the gunfight near Ozona, Crockett County. They had Wells Fargo sacks holding their food. Some Texas Rangers quit to spend time looking for the hidden loot. It appears the gang buried their loot between Sanderson and Ozona, possibly in Crockett County or Terrell County. *See* Washington County, "Southern Pacific Loot," as likely the same story on different sides of the state.

Santiago Mountains Gold

A fortune of gold in mule skins carried by thirteen mules was rumored to have been hidden in the northwest or northeast area of the Santiago Mountains during an Indian attack.

Seminole Bill's Lost Mine

Seminole Bill (Bill Kelly), a half-Black, half-Seminole Indian cowboy, was said to have discovered a gold deposit below Boquillas near old Stillwell's Crossing of the Rio Grande in the summer of 1887. He was only about nineteen and spoke little English, having been raised in Mexico. He worked for brothers Lee, Frank, John and Jim Reagan on their ranch. Seminole Bill said he found the gold deposit while bringing cattle in for branding. They were heading to Bullis Bend. Bill later met a railroad man who proclaimed the ore sample to be very rich. Bill then disappeared from history. The railroad man spent the rest of his life searching unsuccessfully for the mine. In the

Seminole Bill's Lost Mine was reportedly near the Rio Grande in Big Bend National Park. *Library of Congress.*

early 1900s, San Antonio newspapers published articles about prospectors searching for this lost gold deposit. The Reagan brothers wrote about where they believed Seminole Bill got the ore sample. This tale also has a possible location in Mexico across the Rio Grande.

Spanish Cache

Packsaddle Mountain supposedly hides a Spanish buried treasure.

BROWN COUNTY

Buck Harmon Treasure

Outlaw lawman Buck Harmon was killed while cattle rustling in 1886. He reportedly hid $1,000 ($80,000) fifteen miles north of Brownwood in the Jim Ned Settlement before his death.

Cow Pens Gold Coins

See San Saba County.

Mose Jackson Treasure

See Mills County.

BURLESON COUNTY

Plantation Treasure

A gold cache was rumored to have been buried on a plantation near Caldwell.

BURNET COUNTY

Gold Outcrop

See Llano County.

Longhorn Cavern Silver

Several legends exist about Longhorn Cavern, which is now a Texas state park. One legend claimed outlaws, including Sam Bass, used the cave as a hideout. Another legend said Spaniards with forty mule loads of silver were attacked by Indians in the area. The Spaniards hid their silver in the cavern. The cavern has been widely explored.

Lost Spanish Silver Mine

An old Spanish document indicated a silver mine was in an area where Fort Croghan and Burnet would later be built. Some forty mule loads of silver from this mine were reportedly buried when Comanches attacked the Spaniards. *See* Williamson County, "Spanish Miners' Treasure."

McFarland's Lost Mine

In 1902, salesman Samuel Lewis McFarland stopped at the old Burnet–San Saba Crossing on the Colorado River for his horse to get water. The river level was low, so he saw a dark area in the rock below the water. He took some rock samples. He was later told it was horn silver. McFarland didn't return to the site until 1925, but the water was too high. Before he died, he returned to the crossing in 1927 with his grandson Harold Furman, but the water was again too high. Dams later increased the river level, which covered the crossing. This site could be in Lampasas County or Llano County.

Safe in a Well

Near Sudduth, outlaws being chased reportedly dumped a safe containing $40,000 in gold coins down a well.

CALDWELL COUNTY

Lost Clear Fork Silver Mine and Treasure

A lost silver mine was said to be near Lockhart on Clear Fork Creek. Another version of this tale was that raiding Indians in the area loaded a wagon with booty, which included silver. A party of white men pursued the Indians, who were slowed down by the wagon. The Indians dumped the silver into Clear Fork Creek, unhitched the horses from the wagon and fled. About eight miles northwest, the Indians murdered a white woman they had taken captive. She was buried nearby. Her grave was marked and was seen for years afterward. The creek bed has been extensively searched by dredging, seining and probing, with nothing found.

Mexican Smelter Cache

In an old smelter near Luing, a Mexican cache of forty-three silver bars ($33,000) was supposedly hidden in a shaft on top of a hill in a sandy area. This could be in Gonzales County or Guadalupe County.

Santa Anna Lockhart Treasure

In the Lockhart area, another Santa Anna treasure of gold coins was said to have been buried.

CALHOUN COUNTY

Constitution

The American 212-ton steamer *Constitution*, built in 1830, was stranded on January 12, 1838, at Matagorda Bay carrying $35,000 specie, with no loss of life. It could be in Matagorda County.

False Live Oak Point Pirate Cache

At False Live Oak Point, a pirate treasure of gold coins was reportedly cached.

Independence

The American 1,376-ton steamboat *Independence*, built in 1851, was stranded in Matagorda Bay on March 26, 1852, with $225,000 in gold and silver bars. Six lives were lost. It could be in Matagorda County.

Indianola Treasures

Several treasures were claimed to be in the Indianola area. The 1875 and 1886 hurricanes and time destroyed this town on Lavaca Bay. Indianola is now under Lavaca Bay.

Lafitte Lavaca Bay Treasure

After pirate Jean Lafitte left Galveston Island, a legend indicated he cached a $1 million treasure at the mouth of the Lavaca River at Lavaca Bay, maybe on Sand Point. To mark the site, a large brass rod was driven into the ground. A pirate reportedly told this story while dying in New Orleans. A man named Hill bought land where he thought the treasure was hidden. One of Hill's workers, who did not know of the treasure story, saw the brass rod and removed it. Hill and his worker were unable to find where the rod was originally placed. Hill never found the treasure. It could be in Victoria County.

Meteor

This American 542-ton steamship was snagged on April 29, 1852, in Matagorda Bay, carrying $40,000 in specie aboard, with no loss of life. This ship was built in 1851. It could be in Matagorda County.

Mexican Families Treasure

At Tiger Lake on Lavaca Bay, on John Wedig's land, a legend claimed Mexican families hid their gold, silver and other valuables before fleeing south after Santa Anna's defeat at the Battle of San Jacinto in 1836. Four Mexican settlements were said to have been along Lavaca Bay. This treasure could be in Victoria County.

Palmetto

The American 533-ton steamship *Palmetto*, built in 1846, was stranded on January 9, 1851, in Matagorda Bay, with $35,000 in specie and no loss of life. It could be in Matagorda County.

Jean Lafitte's pirates boarded many ships in the Gulf of Mexico and may have cached treasure on the Texas Gulf Coast. *Library of Congress.*

Pirate Chest

See Aransas County.

Santa Rosa

In 1816, the Spanish frigate (brig) *Santa Rosa* sank in Matagorda Bay with a reported $2 million in treasure. There are several stories that pirates plundered the *Santa Rosa* and possibly buried its treasure. It could be in Matagorda County. *See also* Rusk County, "Lafitte Hendricks Lake Treasure."

CALLAHAN COUNTY

Hubbard Creek Treasure

See Shackelford County.

Spanish Treasures

The Coronado Treasure, worth about $60 million, was rumored hidden in an eighty-acre pasture on the Sems Ranch near Clyde. A number of rocks and trees there had marks indicating where the treasure was buried. Another version has Spanish gold, silver and jewels hidden in Alamo Canyon of the Sacramento Mountains near Clyde.

Spider Rock Treasure

Dave Arnold arrived at the Flying H Bar Ranch between Abilene and Cisco telling a strange tale of Spanish treasure, worth millions of dollars, hidden in a tunnel system. Indians had attacked the Spaniards and wiped them out, leaving the treasure behind. On the ranch, there was a series of rocks oriented in a man-made way. Arnold claimed he could decipher the markings to locate the treasure. A flat sandstone rock with carvings on both sides was recovered under an ancient oak. Over several years, Arnold returned to the ranch without finding treasure. Many groups have fruitlessly searched this area for treasure, although Spanish graves, copper suns, knives and other material were recovered. Tom Penfield's *A Guide to Treasure in Texas* has several pages on this story. *See* Stonewall County, "Lost Conquistador Treasures/Spider Rock Treasures," as the same man, Dave Arnold, was associated with that story.

CAMERON COUNTY

Battle of Resaca de la Palma Treasure

At the start of the Mexican War, ferryman Ramon took Mexican soldiers across the Rio Grande near Brownsville. Ramon claimed the Mexican army buried the Mexican general's money chest and silver plates on the Resaca de la Palma battlefield, about three miles from the Rio Grande. The treasure chest was buried in the middle of a triangle formed by three palm trees, and a fire was made over it to hide the location. One soldier who buried it fled, as he feared he and his companions would be murdered. Mexican officers reportedly buried personal items, including any money they had, before the battle. Mexican general Mariano Arista, his silver service and his writing desk were captured by General Zachary Taylor's American army on May 9, 1846, at the Battle of Resaca de la Palma. The Mexican force of about

A legend indicates Coronado's Treasure was hidden near Clyde. *Library of Congress.*

At Resaca de la Palma, the defeated Mexican army reportedly left behind treasure. *Library of Congress.*

4,000 soldiers lost 8 cannons, 154 killed, 205 wounded and 156 missing. American losses were 33 killed and 89 wounded. The Palo Alto Battlefield National Park contains the Mexican camp and covers about one-third of the battlefield.

Cincinnati

This ship sank on May 5, 1853, off Brazos Island with $25,000 in specie aboard.

Clara Woodhouse

This American steamship sank with $80,000 in specie and possibly some silver bullion on November 1, 1877, off Brazos Island on the north breakers sand bar.

Colonel Harvey

During the Mexican War, on October 12, 1846, the 132-ton American steamship *Colonel Harvey* was lost off Brazos Bar with $10,000 in specie. It was built in 1844.

Columbia

This ship sank near Brazos Santiago Pass with $800,000 in 1931.

E.P. Wright

This schooner sank in 1914 near Brazos Santiago Pass with $100,000 in gold and silver and a cargo of guns and ammunition.

Frontier

During the Mexican War, about one mile up the Brazos Santiago Pass off the west end of Padre Island, the 109-ton American steamship *Frontier* was stranded on June 19, 1846, with $210,000 in gold, bullion and specie and a cargo of wine. No loss of life.

Globe

On June 17, 1851, the 481-ton American sidewheel steamer *Globe*, built in 1842, was stranded near Brazos Island with no loss of life, carrying $105,000 in gold and silver specie.

Ida Lewis

This ship sank with $20,000 in specie on June 25, 1875, near the north breakers spit off Brazos Island.

Jessie

In 1875, off the mouth of the Rio Grande, a hurricane sank the American steamer *Jessie* with a treasure of $86,000 to $100,000 on board. It is also said to be off Matamoros, Mexico.

Juan Nepomuceno Cortina Treasure

Juan Nepomuceno Cortina, the Mexican Robin Hood, was rumored to have buried much treasure near his family's ranch at Santa Rita, near Brownsville. He was a powerful Mexican governor, politician, rancher and military man. He engaged in a personal war against south Texas over the years before he died in 1894.

Powerful Mexican landowner, politician and general Juan Cortina supposedly hid treasure on his family's ranch near Brownsville. *Library of Congress.*

Lago de las Pajores Treasure

This treasure was supposed to have been stashed near Brownsville.

Lea

On June 10, 1880, the American steamer *Lea* sank about one-half mile off the mouth of the Rio Grande near Matamoros, Mexico, with $100,0000 in gold and silver specie aboard.

Long Island Treasure

Near the old submerged Mexican town of Bagdad, just outside of Brownsville, on Long Island, a large Confederate money cache was recovered. Bagdad was used for moving goods between Mexico and Confederate Texas during the Civil War.

Lost City Treasure

Lost City was located about twenty-five miles north of the south end of Padre Island. Gold coins in a bushel basket were reportedly recovered below two crossed swords that stuck out of the sand there. This treasure could be in Willacy County. *See* Cameron County/Kenedy County/Willacy County (Padre Island), "John Singer Treasures."

Mexican Army Payroll

A legend has a $250,000 Mexican army payroll buried six miles northeast of Brownsville after the Battle of Palo Alto on May 8, 1846, between General Zachary Taylor's 2,300 American soldiers and General Mariano Arista's 3,700 Mexican soldiers. A relative of a Mexican soldier who fought at the battle claimed his ancestor helped bury seven cartloads of money near a gully or gulch. The soldier feared he would be murdered to hide the treasure site, so he fled the army.

Before the Battle of Palo Alto, Mexican army soldiers supposedly buried treasure. *Library of Congress.*

Mexico

The American 144-ton (or 120-ton) sidewheel steamer *Mexico* was built in 1859 and burned on March 18, 1865, off Port Isabel, with $1,500 in specie aboard and no loss of life.

Miner's Gold

A gold miner returned to the United States from Mexico with several thousand dollars in gold. He went to Padre Island to avoid Indians but was attacked by them there. He reportedly hid his gold and temporarily hid most of his body in the sand to avoid detection. He escaped and never recovered his gold. As he was dying in Corpus Christi around 1900, about twenty years after his adventure occurred, he told this tale.

Reine de Mers

The French brig *Reine de Mers* (*Reine de Mars*) sank on November 15, 1875, inside of Brazos Island. Its cargo included $100,000 in gold and silver specie, as well as wines and liquor.

San Pedro

The Spanish ship *San Pedro*, with 500,000 pesos in gold and silver specie, sank on July 5, 1811, off the west end of Padre Island in Brazos Santiago Pass. Lafitte may have attacked it. Most of the treasure may have been salvaged quickly.

S.J. Lee

On December 6, 1873, the 176-ton American sidewheel steamer *S.J. Lee* was stranded off Brazos Island on a sand bar with $100,000 in gold and silver specie, as well as a small chest with jewels owned by a passenger. Brownsville was also a location given for the wreck. Also said to have sunk in 1875 with $150,000 in gold and silver, a small chest of jewelry and no loss of life. This ship was built in 1866.

The Texas Navy sloop *Austin*, which captured silver bullion off the Yucatán. *U.S. Naval History and Heritage Command.*

Texas Navy Silver Bars

The sloop *Austin* was part of the Texas navy formed to protect Texas and attack Mexican vessels. The *Austin* cruised off the Yucatán Peninsula in 1842, capturing a Mexican schooner carrying two hundred silver bars. The *Austin* took 25 silver bars aboard. The other 175 silver bars sank in the Mexican schooner off Juarez Point, Mexico, in a depth of about 420 feet. The *Austin*'s crew wanted to divide the silver among themselves, but the captain believed the silver was the property of the Republic of Texas. The *Austin* anchored off south Padre Island in a storm. Its captain and a crewman loaded the silver bars in a small boat. On the land side of Padre Island, they cached the silver and made a map of the burial site. Over time, the map was lost, so the treasure was not recovered. It could be in Willacy County.

Texas Ranger

On June 25, 1875, this American schooner sank with $200,000 in gold and silver bars and specie off Brazos Island on a sand spit.

Two Cannons Treasure

Major General Nathaniel Banks's Union troops occupied Brazos Island on November 2, 1863. When four Union soldiers explored Padre Island, they were said to have found two brass cannons filled with Spanish doubloons and pieces of eight.

Wailing Wayne Cache

On Padre Island, $90,000 in gold coins in an old jug was reportedly hidden by Wailing Wayne, who came to Port Isabel in the 1930s with a lot of money. He left for Galveston for a couple of weeks and was never seen again. Some think he hid his cache on south Padre Island, while others think he took it with him.

Yacht

This American 249-ton steamer, built in 1844, was stranded off the Brazos Bar with $1,500 in specie aboard on September 23, 1853, with no loss of life.

CAMERON COUNTY/KENEDY COUNTY/WILLACY COUNTY (PADRE ISLAND)

Capitana of 1552 Fleet

The 1552 Spanish fleet from Veracruz was attacked by pirates a few days out of port. The *capitana* (flagship) of the fleet fought the pirates, while the rest of the fleet headed to safety. The *capitana* was holed and sank with about three hundred aboard, along with about thirty tons of gold and silver. It may have sunk off Padre Island.

Left: This reconstructed Spanish galleon shows how they looked. Spanish galleons with gold and silver were lost off the Texas Gulf Coast. *Library of Congress.*

Below: The sands of Padre Island hide many lost treasures and shipwrecks. *National Park Service.*

Hermit Brothers Treasure

On Padre Island, several miles north of Lost City, two hermit brothers were rumored to have hidden their treasure. The brothers were murdered by a robber looking for their treasure. Before he was executed, the killer was captured and claimed he never found any of the brothers' money.

John Singer Treasures

During a hurricane, John Singer, his wife and their children were shipwrecked on southern Padre Island in the schooner *Alice Sadell*. John Singer and his family survived and bought part of Padre Island from representatives of the original Spanish grantee, Padre Nicolas Balli (or Belli), from whom Padre Island got its name. Padre Nicolas Balli had a ranch and mission called Rancho Santa Cruz, which became the Singer Ranch. The Singer Ranch included the family's house and blacksmith shop. They raised as many as 1,500 cattle. John Singer's brother, Isaac Singer, invented and developed the Singer Sewing Machine.

John Singer reportedly recovered a metal chest with $90,000 worth of jewels, Spanish doubloons and silver coins when digging a house foundation. The Singer children also recovered Spanish coins from old shipwrecks. During the Civil War, when Union soldiers took over the Singer Ranch, the Singers left Padre Island. John Singer went to Port Isabel. Near the Singer ranch house, John Singer's oldest son, Alexander, said the family treasure was cached in four feet of sand. The treasure contained Mrs. Singer's emerald necklace in a screw top jar and $85,000. John Singer and a son were also said to have buried a treasure of $60,000 to $90,000 in gold and silver in a cast iron tub between two scrub oak trees six miles up Laguna Madre from his ranch.

After the death his wife, Joanna, John Singer recovered several of his treasure caches. In 1868, John Singer returned to Padre Island, but could not locate the main treasure, as the markers had disappeared. Alexander Singer was said to have recovered $2,000 of the family's buried treasure, but not the main cache. One of John Singer's sons also searched for the missing caches but died in 1945 without locating more treasure. Money Hill was a high sand dune near Padre Beach or on the north end of Padre Island where John Singer reportedly cached treasure before leaving Padre Island.

In 1931, Charles Hardin claimed he had located Lost City, the site of John Singer's ranch headquarters. He said it was about twenty-six miles north of the south tip of Padre Island jetty near the Cameron County-

Willacy County line and then one-eighth of a mile inland from the Gulf of Mexico. The Padre Island National Seashore Park covers much of the area of these treasures.

Lafitte Padre Island Treasures

There were said to be at least two pirate Lafitte treasures buried on Padre Island. One treasure chest was said to have been near Port Isabel.

Little Fleeta

The American steamer *Little Fleeta* sank in 1874 with $30,000 off Padre Island.

Maria Theresa

The French bark *Maria Theresa* sank in 1880 with $100,000 off Padre Island.

Paisano

The American sidewheel passenger freighter *Paisano* sank in 1875 with $200,000 in silver dollars. It left Brazos Santiago bound for Galveston and vanished without a trace. It may have sunk between the south end of Padre Island and Galveston. There was talk of the crew turning pirates and killing everyone to get the money. This wreck may be off the east tip of St. Joseph Island.

Santa Maria de Guadalupe

The nao *Santa Maria de Guadalupe* sank in 1564 due to a leaky hull. The registered silver was transferred to other ships, but its contraband treasure may not have been transferred. The wreck location is unknown. Potter, in *The Treasure Diver's Guide*, wrote it might be off Padre Island.

Smuggler Cache

A smuggler was said to have hidden gold coins somewhere on Padre Island.

Cass County

Lost Caddo Lead Mine

See Harrison County.

Chambers County

Lafitte Lone Oak Bayou Treasure

Near three large trees on Lone Oak Bayou, pirate Jean Lafitte was said to have hidden a treasure. Several Spanish doubloons dated 1803 were found near Anahuac on Galveston Bay. In 1940, a man tried to get permission from Texas to salvage a sunken Lafitte ship he claimed might have over $12 million worth of treasure.

Lake Miller Treasure

Near Lake Miller, a treasure was rumored to have been buried. One story was that one of pirate Jean Lafitte's ships, possibly the *Pride*, carried five bearskins of gold, which went down with the ship. In 1833, a group of men near Wallisville outlined a wreck in eight feet of water using lengths of pipe. The men were trespassing and were driven off. The area was likely later filled in. *See* Harris County, "The *Pride*'s Treasure."

Lost Lake Treasure

Treasure was said to have been hidden along the north side of Lost Lake near an old fort.

Old River Treasure

See Liberty County.

Spanish Galleon/Pirate Ship Treasure

In Galveston Bay near Anahuac, a Spanish galleon or one of Lafitte's pirate ships with gold, silver and jewelry aboard reportedly sank.

COKE COUNTY

Lost Payroll

A $90,000 gold payroll was supposedly robbed and hidden between three oak trees that formed a *V* about .75 miles from a Colorado River stagecoach crossing. Said to be south of Bronte.

COLEMAN COUNTY

Santa Anna Mountains Treasures

In the Santa Anna Mountains, legends indicated $10 million in gold ore ($10,000 in gold coins) from a Spanish pack train were either cached in a cave or buried. Kiowa chief Santana (Satanta) was killed in an escape attempt from prison in 1878. A legend claimed he was buried on Santa Anna Mountain with several carts of treasure. However, Chief Santana was initially buried in the Huntsville Prison Cemetery before being buried at Fort Sill, Oklahoma. There is no Texas treasure buried with Santana.

COLLIN COUNTY

Spanish Spring Treasure

See Dallas County.

COLORADO COUNTY

Lost Spanish Treasure Cannon

See Lavaca County.

COMAL COUNTY

Shelton Hollow Ledge

See Hays County.

Cooke County

Sam Bass Loot

Another Sam Bass outlaw cache of $200,000 was reportedly hidden near Rosston and Pond Creek. Cove Hollow was also mentioned as where Bass and his gang hid treasure.

Spanish Fort Treasure

See Montague County.

Walnut Bend Treasures

A treasure was rumored to have been hidden near Dexter in the Walnut Bend of the Red River. The Cross Timbers Treasure was also said to be located near Dexter. It could be in Grayson County.

Coryell County

Comanche Treasure

See Lampasas County.

Padre Treasure

In 1832, according to legend, padres buried gold at Gholson's Gap near Evant (Coryell and Hamilton Counties) and a couple of miles north of Adamsville (Lampasas County) between Gholson's Gap and the river.

Snively's Lost Mine

See Val Verde County.

CRANE COUNTY

Castle Gap Treasures/Maximilian Treasure

See Upton County.

Chief Yellow Wolf Treasure

See Ward County.

Two Cannons

See Pecos County.

Wagon Train Treasure

Indians attacked a wagon train southwest of Crane and killed the travelers. A trunk with money and other objects was reportedly buried during the attack.

CROCKETT COUNTY

James Gang Ranch Treasure

See Pecos County.

John Flint Loot

Bass Outlaw, a former Texas Ranger in Ozona, looked for outlaw John Flint's buried treasure near Ozona. Supposedly the Texas Rangers were about to capture John Flint when he committed suicide and left his loot hidden somewhere.

Sanderson Loot

See Brewster County.

Spanish Gold Cave

See Terrell County.

CULBERSON COUNTY

Apache Canyon Treasure

Gold bullion worth $330,000 was supposedly buried in the Sierra Diablo Mountains in Apache Canyon. It could be in Hudspeth County.

Eighteen Mule Loads of Loot

North of Van Horn near Grapevine Springs in the Guadalupe Mountains, eighteen mule loads of loot taken from Mexican churches was said to have been hidden.

Found Gold Bullion

In his book *Treasure Hunter*, W.C. Jameson revealed that in 1953, as a youngster, he was part of a group that retrieved a treasure of fifty gold bars from a cave on a ranch in the Guadalupe Mountains near Juniper Spring.

Hap Sweeney Cache

Cowboy Hap Sweeney found a gold ingot cache in the Guadalupe Mountains in a cave. After Sweeney died, in 1913, his two saddlebags were found in the 1930s, in a burned hollowed-out tree in the Bowl area of Guadalupe Mountains National Park. The saddlebags contained Sweeney's diary, a map and a gold bar. According to his diary, he had found forty gold bars and retrieved just one. W.C. Jameson's *Treasure Hunter* detailed how Jameson happened upon this tale and his search for the treasure.

Jesse and Frank James Buried Loot

Outlaw Jesse James and his brother Frank James owned a ranch in West Texas. Eugene R. Anderson, in a *True Treasure* article, claimed to have located the ranch near the mouth of McKittrick Canyon, which runs through parts of Texas and New Mexico in the Guadalupe Mountains. About 1870, Jesse and Frank James were said to have taken refuge in the area and made a deposit of their ill-gotten gains for later retrieval. Anderson thought it might be about $20,000, buried between two juniper trees near their cabin. This location may be part of the Guadalupe Mountains National Park.

Juniper Springs Treasure Cave

Near Juniper Springs on the upper end of the Rader Ridge in the Guadalupe Mountains, goat shepherd Jesse Duran found a small cave in the spring of 1930. The distance between Rader Ridge and Juniper Springs was said to be about a mile. While Duran was walking on a large flat rock, it slid and revealed the cave. Inside the cave, he reportedly found two (three) skeletons, weapons and several strongboxes full of gold coins. Duran told this tale to his boss, Frank Stogden. Duran feared going back to the cave and moved away. The treasure cave was said to be about fifty miles south of Carlsbad, New Mexico. It is likely in Guadalupe Mountains National Park.

Lost Negro Mine

North of Van Horn is where the Lost Negro Mine was supposed to be located.

Lost San Antone Mine and Treasure

A legend indicated that near Lordsburg, around 1600, Spaniards forced Indians to mine gold. In 1616, the Indians revolted and caused the Spaniards to cache their gold and leave. San Antone and a Spanish expedition from Mexico City returned and mined about $2 million in gold. San Antone died while heading to Mexico with his gold. Indians reportedly killed all the Spaniards but one, who made it back to Mexico City. The mine was located in the headwaters of the Rio Priato (Black River area) in the Guadalupe Mountains in Culberson County or southeastern Otero County, New Mexico. *See* Jeff Davis County, "Lost San Antone Mine," for a different San Antone Mine.

Lost Sublett Mine/Lost De Gailan Mine

Spanish captain Gavilan and thirty Spaniards were supposedly led by an Indian from Tabira (Gran Quivira) to a gold deposit in the eastern

Guadalupe Mountains. At Sierra de las Cenizas (Mountain of the Ashes), the Spaniards discovered gold nuggets. The Pueblo Revolt of 1680 caused the mine to be abandoned.

Ben (Will or William) Sublett came to Odessa with three hungry kids. He was always broke before he found Gavilan's mine. Some thought the mine was in Eddy County, New Mexico. Sublett took ore from his mine to Midland and sold it for $1,500. It took three to four weeks in the Guadalupe Mountains (possibly near Guadalupe Peak, the highest Texas mountain, with an elevation of 8,751 feet) for him to make a round trip and mine ore. Sublett was said to have also sold ore for $1,700 in Galveston. Sublett did his mining from about 1880 to 1892 and later died in Carlsbad, New Mexico. In Howard Clark's *Lost Mines of the Old West*, the story had nuggets (not ore) that Sublett brought back and that were seen by people. He showed the mine to his son Ross (Rolth) and Mike Wilson. Ross said the mine was located in the Rustler Hills and that his father went over a ledge of rock on a rope ladder and returned with a bag of gold from the mine down below. There was a spring at the edge of a deep ravine where Ben left his son with the horses. There are some who believe the mine is a few miles north of Rustler Spring. There are a number of versions of this popular story.

Policarpo Gonzales's Gold

See Hudspeth County.

Quick Killer Silver Mine

See Hudspeth County.

DALLAS COUNTY

Jesse James Loot

Near Dallas, Jesse James was said to have cached $20,000 in gold and silver coins. One version claimed Jesse James and Sam Bass buried a wagon full of loot in an old Spanish mine in Dallas near Chalk Hill. The mine entrance was blown up. There is no evidence Jesse James and Sam Bass ever met.

Outlaw Flagpole Hill Park Cache

An outlaw cache of $16,000 in gold coins was said to have been buried one hundred yards north of the first bridge on the northwest highway west of Flagpole Hill Park in Dallas.

Sam Bass Dallas Area Loot

Outlaw Sam Bass was said to have hidden loot near Dallas, as he was once a cowboy in this area. One cache of $200,000 was reportedly near a forked stump and a spring west of the Trinity River. A pencil-drawn map indicated the treasure was two blocks north of Oak Cliff near the Houston Street Viaduct. Another story has $30,000 in gold coins hidden. Chalk Hill, Schnault Springs in north Dallas and Duck Creek near Dallas are other potential cache sites.

Spanish Spring Treasure

Thirteen carretas of gold, silver and church treasure were rumored to have been pushed into a deep spring near the East Fork of the Trinity River about ten miles northeast of Garland when Indians attacked a Spanish caravan. This treasure could be in Collin County or Rockwall County.

DENTON COUNTY

Blacksmith Cache

Near Lake Lewisville (Lake Garza-Little, Lake Dallas) a blacksmith was said to have hidden $5,000 in $20 gold pieces and silver coins. He died before revealing where it was to his wife or others. According to one story, the blacksmith shop location is now under the lake and the old barn location is along the lakeshore.

Denton Outlaw Loot

Outlaws were rumored to have buried $30,000 near Denton. This could be a Sam Bass treasure.

Lost Longest Lead Mine

See King County.

Sam Bass Denton Treasures

Outlaw Sam Bass was supposed to have buried loot in Denton County. The treasure was said to be $200,000 worth of gold and silver coins. One version was that most of the three thousand newly minted $20 gold pieces from the gang's Union Pacific train robbery at Big Springs, Nebraska, was hidden. Several sites are possible. A saloonkeeper reportedly buried $600 of Sam Bass's $20 gold pieces somewhere in Denton and did not recover them. The newly minted double eagles marked the bandits when they spent some of the money. Posses chased the Bass Gang, with shootouts at Pilot Knob (six miles southwest of Denton), Bullard's Mills and Warner Jackson's Farm (eight miles south of Denton). Other treasure sites mentioned are along Hickory Creek and near Pilot Point in the northwest part of the county.

William Riddle Cache

See Tarrant County.

DICKENS COUNTY

Croton Breaks Lost Silver Mine

This lost mine was said to be near Dickens.

Lost Silver Ledge

A silver ledge was rumored to have been found by buffalo hunters in southern Dickens County or northern Kent County. Indians attacked the hunters, who fled into a canyon and made their way east to Croton Creek. One hunter found blackish rock, which could have been lead. They used it to make bullets. Later, after returning to Mason County, one of the hunters discovered his rock sample was silver. He was going to lead a search party to the ledge but died before he could do so. Some believe it was ten miles north of Gilpin or near Round Mountain, Red Hill or Dickens Hill. It could be in Kent County.

DIMMIT COUNTY

Carrizo Springs Treasure

A cache of gold coins was reportedly hidden at Carrizo Springs.

Espantosa Lake Treasures

Espantosa Lake (Ghostly Lake, Horrible Lake) is about three miles south of Crystal City and north of Carrizo Springs close to the Zavala County-Dimmit County line. A part of Santa Anna's Mexican army was said to have camped here. A cannon with gold (soldiers' coins) in its muzzle was rolled into the lake.

A wagon train loaded with gold and silver also was said to have camped on the lake. That night, the area just sank into the lake. Everyone drowned, and the treasure lies in the lake.

On the upper Presidio Road between Coahuila and the Texas settlements, a Mexican wagon train with several million dollars' worth of gold and silver was about to be attacked by Indians. Near Crystal City, not far from a lake, they reportedly cached the treasure. All were killed but two women, who were held as Indian captives for several years. After being freed, the women led a party to recover the treasure but couldn't locate it.

Outlaws had a hideout at Espantosa Lake, which was raided in August 1876 by Texas Rangers with seven outlaws killed out of thirty.

Grand Rock Water Hole Treasure

According to legend, around 1803, thirty mule loads of gold, silver coins and bullion from Mexico City were being transported to San Antonio under Spanish nobleman Captain Palacio Flores. The party forded the Rio Grande about fifty miles above Laredo, then followed Pena Creek. Robbers attacked the Spaniards at a spring. The treasure was supposedly hidden in the Grand Rock Water Hole of Pena Creek, located several miles northwest of Carrizo Springs. Captain Flores and most of his men died, but the treasure remains. A variation of this tale has it happening in 1700, with Indians attacking the treasure train instead of robbers.

DUVAL COUNTY

Cerro del Rico Cache

A cache of gold and silver coins was supposed to be hidden in the San Diego area.

Rock Pens Treasure

See McMullen County.

Six Mule Loads of Coins

Before bandits attacked, six mule loads of Mexican silver coins worth $300,000 were reportedly cached in a sand dune and well south of Realitos. All the mule handlers were killed in the attack. This treasure could be in Jim Hogg County.

EASTLAND COUNTY

Cisco Robbery

A legend exists that in 1927, eight miles west of Cisco and three miles from US-80 between Cisco and Putnam, the Turgen Gang hid about $36,000 to $38,000 from robberies in Cisco and Abilene. This story is false. On December 23, 1927, two open cars with two robbers in each car stopped in Cisco near the First National Bank of Cisco. Three men entered the bank, one of them wearing a Santa Claus costume. Two Cisco policemen and one robber were killed in the shootout. Records report $12,400 in cash and $150,000 in nonnegotiable securities were taken, but all were recovered and returned to the bank.

ECTOR COUNTY

Chief Yellow Wolf Treasure

See Ward County.

EDWARDS COUNTY

Lost Edwards County Spanish Mines

Spanish silver mines were said to have been located in Edwards County. Indian attacks caused them all to be abandoned.

Mexican Loma Alta Cache

See Val Verde County.

EL PASO COUNTY

El Paso Outlaw Loot

North of El Paso, a gang of train robbers supposedly cached their loot in a cave.

Leach Treasure

Near El Paso, James B. Leach was said to have hidden $250,000 in gold and silver.

Mount Franklin Treasures

A 1616 letter told of Spanish church gold and silver hidden on Mount Franklin. Near La Esmeralda, north of El Paso and on Mount Franklin, a treasure of gold coins was reportedly stashed under a large rock. Padres from Mission Nuestra Señora de Guadalupe de El Paseo were supposed to have had mines in the area and hidden their treasure on Franklin Mountain.

Padre Treasures and the Lost Padre Mine (La Mina del Padre)

A legend indicated 250 to 300 burro loads of Jesuit or padre gold and silver was hidden during the 1680 Pueblo Revolt in a Franklin Mountains mine or possibly ten miles east of El Paso. This treasure was supposedly from Mission Nuestra Señora de Guadalupe in El Paso del Norte, Mexico, across the Rio Grande from El Paso, Texas. One version claimed 4,300 gold bars, 5,000 silver bars and nine mule loads of jewels, vessels and ornaments were

The Franklin Mountains near El Paso have a number of lost treasure and lost mine tales. *National Archives.*

hidden. In 1888, a man called Robinson was said to have found what he thought was the mine and removed material from inside. He ran out of money and stopped digging.

In 1901, L.C. Criss discovered a mine shaft after removing rock covering it. His hired diggers removed 125 feet of material from the shaft. At a *T* with adobe brick blocking both shafts, they stopped, as they needed timber supports. Criss left his workers behind while he went to raise money to buy timber. One worker continued excavating and was killed by a cave-in, which blocked the tunnel. In 1968, another man called Martin, his wife and a helper called McKinney used heavy equipment to excavate rock to look for a mine shaft. Land ownership problems stopped further excavation.

Pancho Villa's Treasures

A cache of gold and silver bars from Pancho Villa's raids was rumored hidden in the Franklin Mountains near El Paso. Franklin Mountain was another area where a Pancho Villa cache could have been hidden. In 1913, Villa was said to have lived on South Orange Street in Little Chihuahua. Villa bought three cars while there. There were several versions of this story, including one in which Villa's aide hid the treasure and the aide died before he could tell anyone where the treasure was. The word "ORO" was supposed to have been cut into a rock as a marker to the treasure. This could be in Mexico.

At one time, Pancho Villa lived in El Paso, so he may have hidden treasure near there. *Library of Congress.*

Rio Grande Cache

See Hudspeth County.

Spanish Silver Coins

A wagonload of Spanish silver coins was supposedly cached at the Piedras Paredes site on the Rio Grande opposite Country Club, northwest of downtown El Paso. The presumed treasure site was later covered by about fifty feet of dirt and rock.

FALLS COUNTY

Hightower Cache

See Limestone County.

FANNIN COUNTY

Mexican Treasure Caches

Around 1844, a Mexican wagon train was reportedly carrying money from Mexico to buy goods in St. Louis. Texas had broken away from Mexico, so the Mexicans in the wagon train were afraid of attack by Texans or bandits. At the Red River, they saw several men riding toward them and thought they were about to be attacked. The Mexicans buried $500 on a hill and put a rock over the location. This was a mile or so from the Red River and near a large cottonwood tree. Proceeding southward, they buried another cache of $500 on another hill. Traveling southward to a third hill, they buried the rest of their money. The wagons were then destroyed. The Mexicans rode their horses back to Mexico. The Mexican War broke out before the Mexicans could return to Texas to retrieve their money. The Mexican traders died, but several groups have reportedly looked for markers of where the money was cached.

FRIO COUNTY

Cassidy's Gold

See Maverick County.

Hogs Found Treasure

J. Frank Dobie's *Legends of Texas* volume 1 reported rooting hogs uncovered four hundred Mexican coins in the 1880s in Frio County.

GALVESTON COUNTY

Barber's Hill Treasure

On Galveston Island's Barber's Hill, boxes with gold and jewels were rumored to have been cached.

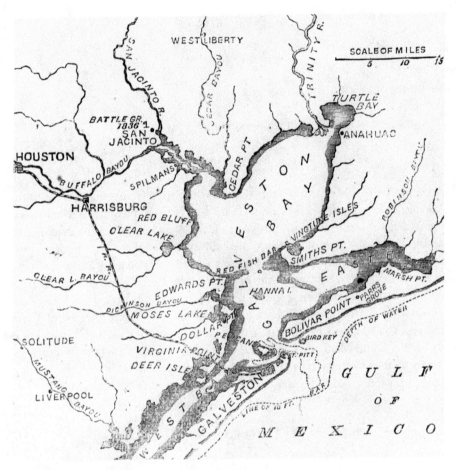

An 1863 Galveston Bay map. *U.S. Naval History and Heritage Command.*

1818 Hurricane Shipwrecks

The September 12, 1818 hurricane wrecked a number of vessels midway between the east end of Galveston Island and Pelican Island. Two wrecks were located south of Bolivar Point about three hundred yards offshore. Four ships were wrecked on the north end of Galveston Island off Virginia Point.

Five Spanish Ships

On September 4, 1766, during a hurricane, five Spanish ships were wrecked on Galveston Island. These shipwrecks included *El Nuevo Constante* and *La*

Caraquena (Guipuzcuana). The majority of the passengers and crew survived, and most of the treasure was salvaged.

Grapeshot

The American 179-ton sidewheel steamer *Grapeshot* burned on May 8, 1858, in Galveston Bay with $2,000 in specie and no loss of life. This ship was built in 1855. It could be in Harris County.

Hans Washington Treasure

On Galveston Island, Hans Washington reportedly cached $1 million worth of gold coins.

Holt's Treasure

See Brazoria County.

Lafitte's Grove Treasure

Another legend about pirate Jean Lafitte indicated he buried a chest of gold and coins at Lafitte's Grove. He marked the site with a brass rod. It was said to have been located about fifty yards east of Steart's Road, about twelve miles down island.

Lively

The schooner *Lively* contained settlers and supplies for Stephen F. Austin's Anglo-American Texas colony when wrecked off Galveston Island's west end near San Luis Pass in 1822. No lives were lost, so most of the cargo and treasure would have been recovered. It could be in Brazoria County.

Mascatee Treasure

The Mascatee Treasure was reportedly $130,000 in specie cached in the early 1800s on Galveston Island near Bolivar Point opposite Lafitte's Maison Rouge. This may be another pirate Jean Lafitte treasure. The word "Mascatee" was said to be related to Lafitte's pirates. Filibuster James Long planned to look for the treasure before he died in a Mexican prison in 1822. Long had seized one of Lafitte's small craft and reported hearing of the treasure in an 1820 letter he wrote to General E.W. Ripley.

Old Woman's Treasure

An elderly recluse lived in the middle of Galveston Island. She supposedly buried gems and jewelry in a jar near her house. She suddenly died, and no one knew where she hid her treasure.

Pelican Island Treasure

In 1970, treasure hunters requested permission from the Galveston City Council to hunt for a $27 million treasure said to be on Pelican Island. Pelican Island was a sand spit that was expanded by dredge material into four thousand acres in Galveston harbor.

Sabine

The *Sabine* was carrying Texas immigrants when it sank about sixty yards off Lafitte's Grove (three lone trees) on Galveston Island on December 22, 1834, with unknown cargo.

GONZALES COUNTY

Mexican Smelter Cache

See Caldwell County.

GRAYSON COUNTY

Jesse James Pottsboro Loot

Near Pottsboro, outlaw Jesse James was said to have hidden $40,000 in loot from a robbery of the Texas State Fair ticket office in Dallas. With Texas Rangers in pursuit, he reportedly buried his loot between a large flat rock and a pine tree before going to Indian Territory (Oklahoma). The reported site near the Red River may now be under Lake Texoma.

Several outlaw treasures were said to have been hidden near the Red River in north Texas. *National Archives.*

Walnut Bend Treasures

See Cooke County.

GREGG COUNTY

Dalton Gang Loot

The Bill Dalton gang robbed the First National Bank in Longview on May 23, 1894. One outlaw and a bystander died, and three others were wounded in a gunfight. The outlaws made off with a reported $2,000 in cash, as well as unsigned bank notes. They may have hidden some loot near Longview during their escape. It could be in Harrison County.

GRIMES COUNTY

Train Robbery Loot

See Terrell County.

Guadalupe County

Mexican Smelter Cache

See Caldwell County.

Hamilton County

Padre Treasure

See Coryell County.

Hardin County

Bad Luck Creek Lost Gold Coins

See Polk County.

Cave of Treasure

See Jasper County.

Harris County

Buried Mexican Payroll

See Waller County.

Cannons Treasure

Two cannons with gold hidden in their barrels were rumored to be underwater in Buffalo Bayou not far from Lynchburg. Another variation of this story has them hidden at the mouth of Cedar Bayou.

Dead Man's Lake Treasure

At Dead Man's Lake near Humble, a Mexican wagon train of gold bullion supposedly worth $1 million was attacked about 1830. Only one Mexican survived. He drew a map of where they hid the gold. The survivor gave the map to the doctor who took care of him before the survivor died. Later, the doctor's family looked for the gold but never found it.

Enoch Brinson Treasure

At Brinson's Point on San Jacinto Bay near Morgan's Point, Enoch Brinson operated a ferryboat landing. When Santa Anna's Mexican army advanced on this area in 1836, Brinson reportedly cached his treasure on the west side of La Porte near a grove of trees. Brinson was killed in a fight with Santa Anna's troops.

Grapeshot

See Galveston County.

Lafitte La Porte Treasure

One of Lafitte's treasures was said to have been hidden under an old house at La Porte. Was said to be opposite Bay Ridge. Lafitte's ghost guards his treasure, according to folklore.

Lafitte Seabrook Treasure

Another one of pirate Jean Lafitte's treasures was possibly hidden below some trees near Seabrook.

Piney Point Treasure

Afraid Union forces would confiscate his money, a rich rancher was rumored to have hidden $18,000 in gold at Piney Point, located just west of Houston. When the Civil War was over, the rancher forgot the exact location where he hid the gold, and he couldn't retrieve it.

The Pride's Treasure

In Trinity Bay on the west side of the Morgan's Point ferry landing, pirate Jean Lafitte's flagship *Pride* supposedly sank. One legend has five bearskins of gold aboard. The wreck may have been only two hundred feet from the bank of a twenty-foot-wide channel between Lake Charlotte and the Trinity River. A legend has Lafitte murdering the two men who helped cache the treasure. One story claimed a house was built over the cache to hide it. During a 1950 dredging near Morgan's Point, old ship's timbers were recovered. *See* Chambers County, "Lake Miller Treasure."

Santa Anna's San Jacinto Treasure

According to legend, after the Texans defeated Mexican president and general Antonio Lopez de Santa Anna's army on April 21, 1836, at San Jacinto, twelve thousand pesos in the Mexican army pay chest was hidden. Some believed

Santa Anna had less than twelve thousand pesos when he invaded Texas. After the Battle of San Jacinto, Santa Anna's captured money was reportedly divided up among the victorious Texans. Some indicated Santa Anna also buried a chest of gold before the Battle of San Jacinto.

General Antonio Lopez de Santa Anna reportedly hid his army's payroll before the Battle of San Jacinto in 1836. *Library of Congress.*

Silver Cloud

The sternwheel steamboat *Silver Cloud* sank on October 2, 1866, in Buffalo Bayou, carrying $22,500 of specie aboard, which was likely salvaged or removed.

Harrison County

Confederate Treasure

A legend claimed a Confederate treasure was buried at Marshall during the Civil War. The Confederate Missouri government set up its administrative offices at 402 South Bolivar and its temporary governor's mansion at 109 East Crockett Street after being driven out of Missouri and Arkansas by Union forces. The refugee Missouri government dissolved when the Confederate Trans-Mississippi West Department surrendered in May 1865.

A gold-handled cane was said to have been stuck in the ground to mark the site of a Confederate treasure in Marshall. In 1884, well diggers dug up a gold-handled walking stick at a depth of twenty-four feet with the inscription "From W.H.H. to J.C.C." There was speculation that the treasure had been removed years before and the cane was left behind.

Dalton Gang Loot

See Gregg County.

Lost Caddo Lead Mine

Caddo Indians traded lead in Shreveport for supplies. It was thought the Caddos' lead mine was near Caddo Lake or possibly in Cass County (near John's Creek, Caddo Lake or northeastern Harrison County) or Marion County. A hunter was rumored to have found a mine shaft containing galena but could not find his way back to the mine. This legend covers a very large area.

HASKELL COUNTY

Lost Conquistador Treasures/Spider Rock Treasures

See Stonewall County.

HAYS COUNTY

Minometer Treasure

A gold coins treasure was rumored to be hidden near Dripping Springs.

Shelton Hollow Ledge

Reportedly southwest of Wimberly in Shelton Hollow, a ledge of silver was said to have been found and lost by L.J. Daily (and a friend, in one version) while hunting. Daily climbed a bluff after his dogs and broke off a piece of rock, which he put in his pocket. A week or so later, he recognized it to be high grade silver ore. He returned to the area but could not find the right bluff. It could be in Comal County.

Spanish Pack Train Treasure

On the Old Spanish Trail, a Spanish pack train was supposedly carrying gold bars bound for St. Louis. Knowing they were about to be attacked by outlaws, the Spaniards reportedly buried five chests or hid them in a cave along Onion Creek. One bandit who attacked the pack train at Arroyo de los Garrapatas (Onion Creek) later admitted to a priest while dying that he was part of the gang that attacked and killed the Spaniards. The bandits did not find the hidden gold. It could be in Blanco County.

HEMPHILL COUNTY

Aztec Sun God and Other Gold

In 1910, a man called Sisney searched on the George Griffis Ranch, some ten miles south of Higgin, for an Aztec gold sun god statue and gold coins ($40,000) reportedly hidden by Mexicans and Indians. A Kiowa (Sioux) band attacked the group, so their treasure was supposedly hidden in the sandy edge of a water hole (spring). Sisney never found anything. This treasure could be in Ellis County, Oklahoma.

Paymaster Cache

See Wheeler County.

HILL COUNTY

Hooker's Cave Treasure

A cabin or stagecoach station about eleven miles south of Hillsboro was said to be near Hooker's Cave, which supposedly hid treasure. Coins have been recovered from the area near the old stagecoach station and a nearby creek. About 1900, Ben Loflin came to Robert Hooker's farm and got permission to prospect. After pacing from various markers, Loflin hired a work party. Blasting away a large rock revealed a tunnel and a cave. About one hundred yards into the cave, Hooker and Loflin got into a dispute over the split of any found treasure, so Loflin left. Hooker did not find any gold and reportedly dynamited the cave shut. Another version of this story was that maybe the men found something before Loflin left. The location was near the McLennan County and Hill County line on the Hooker Farm, about twenty-two miles northwest of Waco.

Nolan's Lost Money

In March 1801, Phillip Nolan entered Spanish Texas from Natchez, Mississippi, to buy horses and catch wild horses for resale in the United States. He had a party of twenty-four to twenty-seven men, including Americans, Spaniards and slaves. They captured about three hundred wild mustangs. Nolan had money to buy horses from Spaniards, but he was said not to have spent any, since they had captured so many wild horses. They camped on what became known as the Nolan River upstream of Mustang Creek at what became Battle Branch near the present Live Oak Cemetery. They had a small fort or trading post with corrals. On March 21 or 22, 1801, a party of Spanish soldiers from Nacogdoches under Lieutenant Miguel Musquiz, commanding about ninety regulars and fifty militia with one swivel gun, attacked them. The Spaniards claimed Nolan was a spy gathering information for an American invasion. The Spanish authorities likely viewed Nolan and his party as trespassing on Spanish soil and stealing horses. The outnumbered horse traders quickly were overrun. Nolan was shot and his two slaves, Caesar and Robert, buried his money south of the camp, according to stories. Nolan was helped across Nolan Creek, where he died. Nolan was buried under the largest tree in the region. All the other Americans were captured. One was hanged in Chihuahua, Mexico, in 1807. The rest were said to have died while in Spanish prisons, except for Ellis Bean, who finally made it back to the United States. The slaves who buried the money were said to have been released and likely did not return to the area. Nolan's grave is just northeast of the Highway 174 Nolan River Bridge, with Battle Creek and Live Oak Cemetery to the west on the Nolan River.

HOPKINS COUNTY

William Low's Gold

In 1893, William Low's treasure of $60,000 in gold coins in saddlebags was supposedly hidden near a creek between Commerce and Sulphur Springs. The treasure was within a half-day buggy ride from Commerce.

HOWARD COUNTY

Cistern Loot

See Martin County.

Padre Crosses

On Signal Mountain just southeast of Big Spring, a legend indicated three Spanish padres were buried with their three gold crosses.

HUDSPETH COUNTY

Apache Canyon Treasure

See Culberson County.

Geronimo's Lost Gold Mine

Apache Indian chief Geronimo claimed to know where a gold deposit was in the Guadalupe Mountains. He got gold from it for trading with whites from time to time. Eventually he had the mine filled in. He talked about it while a prisoner of the U.S. Army at Fort Sill, Oklahoma (then Indian Territory), and tried to get guards to release him so he could show them the gold's location. It could be in New Mexico. *See* "Policarpo Gonzales's Gold," as it may be the same mine.

Apache chief Geronimo, who claimed he had a hidden gold mine, with some of his warriors. *Library of Congress.*

Lost Eagle Mountain Mine

A lost gold mine was said to have been in the Eagle Mountains near Eagle Ford or about five miles north of Allamoore.

Policarpo Gonzales's Gold

In 1926, Policarpo Gonzales claimed there was a gold deposit in the Guadalupe Mountains. This is another one of J. Frank Dobie's tales. As payment for restoring his hearing and helping him hear music, a Mexican man led a San Antonio doctor to a site in the Guadalupes and told him to dig forty-five feet from this spot to get the gold. The doctor never did. Gonzales had been brought up by a Fort Stockton army officer and was friendly to the Apaches. The Apaches showed Gonzales a cave, where they retrieved gold to trade with. Later they filled up the cave entrance with forty-five feet of material. This may have been Geronimo's Lost Gold Mine. It could be in Culberson County or New Mexico.

Quick Killer Silver Mine

Major John C. Cremony wrote that an Indian named Quick Killer (Tats-ah-das-ay-go) told him that all the silver he wore came from a silver deposit in the Guadalupe Mountains. While guiding Major Cremony on a scout, Quick Killer revealed the silver deposit's location. Most think it was near the Hudspeth County-Culberson County line just south of New Mexico. It could be in Culberson County or New Mexico.

Rio Grande Cache

On the Rio Grande, about forty miles south of El Paso, a cache of gold and jewels was rumored to have been hidden. It could be in El Paso County.

Victorio's Treasure Cave

W.C. Jameson's book *Buried Treasures of the American Southwest* has a tale about Chief Victorio's Lost Gold, which details a story he got from a teacher interested in western lore. The teacher had interviewed a vagrant prospector who was closing in on Apache chief Victorio's cache of gold bars and other treasure he thought was hidden in a cave in the Eagle Mountains near Indian

Hot Springs. Indian Hot Springs had been used for centuries as a gathering place for Indians and then others. Victorio's treasure was from his many raids in Mexico and the United States. When he needed to trade for guns, ammunition and other supplies, Chief Victorio took gold and silver from his cache. Apaches captured Joe Peacock at the Eagle Springs stage station. He later escaped Apache captivity after being informed about Victorio's secret treasure cave. He spent years looking unsuccessfully for it.

Hunt County

Bois D'Arc Crossing Gold

Near Bois D'Arc Crossing on the Sabine River, about seventeen miles south of Greenville, gold was rumored to have been cached.

William Low's Gold

See Hopkins County.

Hutchinson County

Lost Pot of Gold Coins

A pot of gold was said to have been hidden near a spring and a willow tree west of Borger. It could be in Moore County.

Irion County

Indian Treasure

An Indian treasure was supposedly hidden between two peaks southeast of the Middle Concho River.

Jack County

Cambren Family Cache/Wagon Train Gold

During the spring of 1857, Comanches and Comancheros raided the Jacksboro (then called Mesquiteville) area. The Cambren and Mason

Frontier cabins dotted the Texas frontier. Hostile Indian raids sometimes left settler treasure hidden. *Library of Congress.*

families had adjacent houses on their ranches for protection in the Blue Hills northwest of Jacksboro near Spy Knob. Comanches and Comancheros killed both families during the raid, except for a young Mason boy they took prisoner. The money hidden by the Mason family was taken by the attackers, but about $1,000 hidden by the Cambren family was not found by them. The Comanches and Comancheros then attacked a wagon train coming from California with gold (worth maybe $50,000 or more today) near Spy Knob. The gold had been hidden and all but one of the people in the wagon train were murdered. The survivor reached present-day Jacksboro. Texas Rangers (including Charles Goodnight) and a posse went after the raiders. At the Little Wichita River, the rangers and the posse caught up with the raiders and rescued the young Mason boy while killing several Comanches. The Mason boy recounted the story of the lost treasure.

Mexican Crown

The Mexican crown was said to be in Jack County.

Sam Bass Loot

More Sam Bass loot was claimed to be hidden near Jacksboro at Black Springs.

Spanish Gold Kegs

Beneath an overhang in a canyon about fifteen miles north of Jacksboro, Spaniards supposedly cached three kegs of gold coins.

JACKSON COUNTY

Lafitte Garcitas Creek Treasure

Pirate Jean Lafitte and his men were said to have cached treasure chests (sacks of treasure) on Garcitas Creek (Cox Creek) near the Lavaca River. Lafitte and his men breakfasted with an old couple who lived there, who later told this tale.

Lafitte Lavaca Treasures

In the 1820s, Pirate Jean Lafitte supposedly cached treasure next to two groups of trees called Mauldin and Kentucky Mottes, up the Lavaca River, one-quarter mile east of a shipwreck. Another Lafitte treasure was reportedly near Lavaca Bay and Lolita. It could be in Victoria County. *See* Calhoun County, "Lafitte Lavaca Bay Treasure" for a similar story.

Silver Bars Lavaca Cache

See Lavaca County.

JASPER COUNTY

Cave of Treasure

A cave in a tall bluff overlooking the Neches River reportedly contains treasure hidden by Mexicans after Santa Anna's defeat at the Battle of San Jacinto. The cave entrance was sealed off by a large flat stone with a hole in the center. A map supposedly showed the treasure cave location. It could be in Hardin County.

Indian Gold Mine

See Tyler County.

Lost Lead Mines

In the McKim Hills, Mark Veatch mined lead, which settlers used to make bullets. After Veatch's death, several other men also mined lead there. The son of one of these miners looked for the mine in 1947 but never found it. George B. Hamilton's article in *Treasure World* discussed how he found only traces of lead ore. Lead has been found at several places in the region. This mine could be in Newton County. Also see Sabine County, "Lost Lead Mine."

JEFF DAVIS COUNTY

Confederate Gold

See Reeves County.

Ebony Cross Treasure

Gold coins were supposedly cached near Valentine. This treasure could be in Presidio County.

El Muerto Springs Loot

Gold from a wagon was said to have been buried near El Muerto Springs by the Jim Hughes-Curly Bill Gang and Juan Estrada's bandits. Thomas Penfield detailed this story in *A Guide to Treasure in Texas*. This could be an outlaw treasure of $1.25 million to $3 million. The two gangs combined to rob a mint, smelter and church in Monterrey, Mexico. They were said to have buried most of the silver and jewelry in a twelve-foot-deep hole at El Muerto Springs. The Jim Hughes-Curly Bill Gang then murdered the Mexican bandits. They took some treasure to tide them over. Six or seven years later, the tale was that they brought a wagonload of loot and miners constructed a treasure vault eight-five feet into rock. They filled the entrance with sixty-five feet of cement and killed the miners. Supposed to be in the area of a stage station called El Muerto about thirty-five miles west of Fort Davis in the Davis Mountains. Another treasure site was said to be seventeen miles east of Barrel Spring.

La Mina Perdida Treasure

See Presidio County.

One lost San Antone Mine was supposedly near Fort Davis. *Library of Congress.*

Lost San Antone Mine

This lost mine supposedly was near Fort Davis. A different Lost San Antone Mine was said to be in Culberson County.

Spaniards Revolution Treasure

In Pinto Canyon, twenty-three miles southeast of Van Horn, there was a legend that Spaniards escaping Mexico during a revolution hid their treasure before returning to Spain.

JEFFERSON COUNTY

Lafitte Neches River Treasure

Another legendary pirate Jean Lafitte treasure was hidden near Port Neches and the Neches River in swampy land. Spanish warships chased a Lafitte pirate ship up the Neches River. Its crew buried their treasure. Another version of this story was told about a settler on Shell Ridge named Neil McGaffey. McGaffey lived with his wife and kids in a house about two miles from the Gulf of Mexico. About 1830, a man looking for the treasure stayed with them. The man had been on the pirate ship, which was crewed by thirty-eight men. They had gold and silver looted from a Spanish ship when a hurricane damaged their ship. After weeks of drifting, a storm forced their ship onto Shell Ridge. By then, most of the crew members were dead.

The man said he was one of five surviving crew members. They put a large treasure chest into a hole they dug on Shell Ridge. To mark the site, brass spikes were driven into driftwood. Only the man and the ship's lieutenant made it to New Orleans, where they acquired a sloop. The man killed the lieutenant but was wounded in the fight. It had been four years since the treasure was cached, so he could not find the site. The man said he would split the treasure with McGaffey for help in recovering the treasure. The man left for New York and claimed he would return but never did. McGaffey searched for and finally found the treasure chest.

McGaffey transferred the treasure into three smaller chests he cached at three different locations. Keeping some gold and silver, McGaffey drove his cattle to New Orleans, sold the cattle and headed home with his slave and pack horse. McGaffey became ill and died before he could recover the rest of the treasure and take his family to live in Ireland. His wife never knew where the three smaller treasure chests were buried. They could be in Orange County.

Sabine Pass Treasures

Several treasures were supposedly hidden near Sabine Pass and Port Arthur. These include at least one pirate treasure.

JIM HOGG COUNTY

Rock Pens Treasure

See McMullen County.

Six Mule Loads of Coins

See Duval County.

JIM WELLS COUNTY

Casa Blanca Treasures

Several treasures were rumored hidden near Casa Blanca, which is two miles southwest of Sandia on what was originally a large Spanish land grant. Casa Blanca was a Spanish fort and mission. A sheepherder reportedly later settled there. Mexican bandits invaded Casa Blanca, stealing sheep, torturing the sheepherder to learn where his money was hidden, then killing him. The

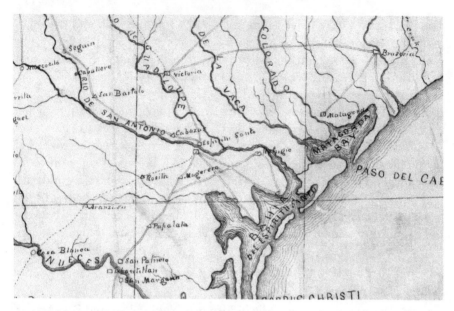

An 1845 Mexican Texas Gulf Coast map. *National Archives.*

bandits hid their loot and were all killed by other outlaws. Near Casa Blanca, $40,000 in gold and silver coins was reportedly buried. One treasure was supposedly hidden near a lake near Lipantitlan, which is southeast of Casa Blanca. In 1807, a treasure was supposed to have been hidden on the Casa Blanca land grant between Laredo Crossing and Corpus Christi Bay.

KARNES COUNTY

Helena Treasures

Several treasures were said to have been hidden in the Helena area along the San Antonio River and the Chihuahua Trail. The Chihuahua Trail was used to move mined silver from Chihuahua to Texas ports.

KAUFMAN COUNTY

Found Spanish Treasure

A Dallas treasure hunter found about three hundred Spanish coins from the mid-1800s in Kaufman County.

Kenedy County

Carreta Trail Treasure

A trail heading north from near Brownsville was used to send pay to the Spanish presidios to the north. Gold coins worth $125,000 were reportedly cached near Armstrong when Indians were about to attack.

Lafitte Point of Rocks Treasure

See Kleberg County.

Sponge Silver

Hundreds of silver bars were reportedly found and lost in the 1950s in Baffin Bay. They may be in Kleberg County.

Kent County

Lost Conquistador Treasures/Spider Rock Treasures

See Stonewall County.

Lost Longest Lead Mine

See King County.

Lost Silver Ledge

See Dickens County.

Kerr County

Lopez Silver

Around 1847, trader Antonio Lopez and a trading party left San Antonio for Santa Fe, New Mexico. They were said to have had pack animals carrying $30,000 ($39,000) in silver coins in leather bags. After the party went past

Bandera Pass, Indians attacked them at Elm Pass. The two surviving traders reportedly cached the silver near the Bandera County-Kerr County line south of Center Point.

KIMBLE COUNTY

Bullion Cache

A sutler left behind at Fort McKavett reportedly saw Indians leave a cedar brake. He went to look at where they had been and found a twenty-foot-deep hole. The sutler went down into the hole by using a rope tied to a tree. He saw a skeleton and a stack of silver bullion at the bottom of the hole. He marked the location so he could find his way back and recover the silver bars. A wildfire destroyed his markers before the sutler could return. This cache could be in Menard County.

A bullion cache was reportedly found and lost by a sutler at Fort McKavett. *Library of Congress.*

Yellow Wolf's Lost Mine

See Llano County.

KING COUNTY

Lost Conquistador Treasures/Spider Rock Treasures

See Stonewall County.

Lost Longest Lead Mine

This lost lead mine was supposed to be near North Croton Creek. Georgian Thomas Longest was in Texas with Luke Callaway to acquire horses. Callaway returned to Georgia, but Thomas Longest continued looking for cattle to buy so he could send big cattle horns home to a friend. Up Croton Creek, he was hit by a sudden storm and took shelter at a bluff in a canyon. He found old mining activity and blackish ore there. Thinking it was silver, he acquired a sample and left. It turned out to be lead. Before he could return, he died. This mine could be in Dickens County, Kent County or Stonewall County.

KINNEY COUNTY

Los Moros Creek Silver Mine

A lost silver mine was rumored to be near Los Moros Creek.

Lost Ana Cacho Mountains Treasure

The Ana Cacho (Anacacho) Mountains were said to contain hidden treasure. It could be in Uvalde County.

Santiago Treasure

Near Spofford, gold bullion and coins were rumored to be hidden in a cave.

KLEBERG COUNTY

Cinenia Caches/Pancho Villa Treasures

Near Cinenia, a Pancho Villa treasure (part of $1.5 million in five caches) of four saddlebags full of gold coins was supposedly buried between four desert patches of ground. This tale was according to Delores Agilero Vasquez, who was seventy-six when she gave a sworn deposition in the Imperial County Hospital at El Centro, California. A $2 million Pancho Villa treasure was also said to have been hidden near Kingsville. *See* Bexar County, "Pancho Villa Treasures"; Nueces County, "Pancho Villa Treasures"; and Starr County, "Pancho Villa Treasure."

Lafitte Point of Rocks Treasure

At Point of Rocks in Baffin Bay, pirate Jean Lafitte's treasure was supposedly buried. The location was rumored to be marked by a copper stake in a rock. This could be in Kenedy County.

Sponge Silver

See Kenedy County.

Spanish Shipwreck Treasure

About twenty miles south of the north tip of Padre Island, a Spanish vessel reportedly wrecked. The survivors were said to have cached treasure in three places on Padre Island before Indians killed them. In the late 1700s, one cache was recovered. Old coins have been found in that area.

LAMAR COUNTY

Eleven Burro Loads of Gold

In northwestern Lamar County, Indians attacked Mexicans herding eleven burros carrying gold on the Spanish Road. These traders may have been carrying gold from a successful trade in either New Mexico or Louisiana. One version of this legend has them throwing their gold into a lake, which could be Palmer Lake. One article claimed it was worth $25,000; another article claimed $75,000 but had no indication it was thrown in a lake. Three of the party escaped to Louisiana. One survivor made a map of the location. Over the years, including 1882, many looked for the gold.

Lost Cauldron of Gold

Near Paris, a slave was said to have helped bury gold coins, gold ingots and silver ingots in a three-legged wash cauldron under a leaning tree on Pine Creek just before the Civil War. After 1900, the former slave told James William Oscar about the cache. In 1924, Oscar and a man with a mineral rod looked for the treasure but did not find it.

Tigertown Rabbit Hole Treasure

Philip R. Rutherford's article in *Treasure Search* revealed a potential outlaw cache of gold bullion located southeast of Tigertown. In the late 1800s, two or three outlaws crossed into Texas from Indian Territory to Tigertown and acted suspicious. The outlaws headed east and then cut south. U.S. marshal Henry Miller and a posse intercepted them southeast of Tigertown and arrested them. The outlaws had seen the lawmen approaching, hid their gold bullion in a rabbit hole and covered the opening. The outlaws were arrested and sent to prison. Henry Miller bought the land where the treasure was said to have been hidden and looked for the treasure unsuccessfully.

LAMPASAS COUNTY

Beasley Cave Ore

See San Saba County.

Comanche Treasure

Comanches were rumored to have stashed $3 million in silver ore and money in a cave near Adamsville.

Comanche Indians made many Texas raids and were said to have hidden their loot. *Library of Congress.*

Lometa Cache

A $50,000 cache of gold coins was supposedly hidden near Lometa.

McFarland's Lost Mine

See Burnet County.

Padre Treasure

See Coryell County.

San Saba Junction Treasure

See San Saba County.

LA SALLE COUNTY

Las Chuzas Mine and Treasure

See McMullen County.

Lost Estambel Hill Treasures

A few miles down the Nueces from Fort Ewell on Rancho de los Olmos, a mule load of gold was reportedly buried. Another version of this story claimed it was $112,000 in Mexican gold. In another variation, a don was said to have hidden thirty-one mule loads of silver near Estambel Hill. Treasure hunters found charcoal, saddles, blankets, burro bones, human bones, but no treasure near a pen there. It could be in McMullin County.

Mexican Army Treasure

A party of Mexican troops were reportedly transporting money when they learned of Santa Anna's defeat at San Jacinto. At the Laredo-San Antonio Crossing on the Nueces River, the soldiers buried the money, as

Some Texas treasures were hidden by ranchers after selling their cattle herds. *Library of Congress.*

they believed Texans were approaching. They burned the wagon over the burial spot to hide the treasure site. A survivor later came back and found an empty hole, a few scattered coins and old leather bags that once held the treasure.

Musgraves Gold

Musgraves was said to have received $12,000 in Mexican gold coins for selling cattle. He left Cotulla bound for San Antonio to deposit the money in a bank. Outside of Cotulla, he got drunk, buried his money and forgot where he hid it.

Revolution Treasure

A legend claimed a treasure was buried near Time. During the 1811 Mexican revolt, a group of revolutionaries fleeing Coahuila crossed the Rio Grande and were rumored to have buried coins and bullion between Cotulla and Artesia Wells south of the Nueces River. The revolutionaries all died and never got their treasure.

Rock Pens Treasure

See McMullen County.

Seven Rocks Hill Silver

See McMullen County.

LAVACA COUNTY

Lost Dutchman Lead Mine

This Lost Dutchman Mine was reportedly a lead mine located near Halletsville. Dutchman or German Frank Vanlisten was said to have found the deposit and mined it. He lived on the Lavaca River near the Gulf Coast. Vanlisten was found dead, possibly from suicide or murder. No one knew where his mine was.

Lost Spanish Treasure Cannon

A cannon barrel full of treasure (gold) was said to have been cached on Big Sandy Creek during the War of Texas Independence. This story was told to Roscoe Martin by a Mexican veteran of the war named White. The cannon could be in Colorado County or Wharton County.

Silver Bars Lavaca Cache

Near a bank of the Lavaca River, silver bars were supposedly cached. They could be in Jackson County.

LEE COUNTY

James Goacher's Lead Mine

About 1835, James Goacher came to Texas to live near Giddings on Rabb's Creek. He mined lead nearby and supplied settlers with lead for their bullets. His lead mine had been originally used by Indians. Indians attacked him and his family. The men were all killed, and the women were taken captive. Years later, Dr. John M. Johnson's wife found a peculiar rock in the area;

the Johnsons used the rock as a doorstop. Upon finding the rock was almost pure lead, Mrs. Johnson tried unsuccessfully to find the deposit where she had picked it up.

LIBERTY COUNTY

Big Thicket Cache

A legendary cache of $1.5 million in church treasure and jewelry was supposed to be in a copper treasure chest. It was hidden on the edge of Big Thicket northwest of Liberty at the base of Halfway Hill not far from Kenefik (Kennifluk). In the 1930s, sharecropper Ben Barney and his wife, Ella, found two 30-inch-long wooden rods covered with beaded leather. They used the beads to make a necklace. Later, two visitors who appeared to be priests came to their house asking about treasure, then left. The Barneys were frightened and went to neighboring farmer Jed Murphy. Using a steel rod, Murphy hit a solid object at around seven feet in the nearby swamp. With a block and tackle and mules, they placed chains around the copper chest and pulled it to the surface. Using a pick to open the chest, they saw jeweled knives, crosses and other treasure. The wooden tripod holding the block and tackle failed. The chest fell back into the swamp. They were unable to retrieve the chest. The landowner later found out about the treasure and got experts involved, who were unable to find the treasure chest. *See* "Spanish Mule Train Treasure," which is similar.

Old River Treasure

Near Old River, a treasure was said to have been hidden near a cedar tree, now cut down. It could be in Chambers County.

Spanish Mule Train Treasure

A legend indicated a Spanish twelve-mule train transported about 3,600 pounds of gold down the Old Spanish Trail (parallel to US-90). On Bowie Creek near the present town of Dayton, the Spaniards were attacked. A northeast to southwest trench was supposedly dug at the Jameson Place, with mules and human remains buried in it. A big copper chest with gold was reportedly buried in one end of the trench. An oak tree was marked to indicate the treasure location. The tree was later cut down.

Treasure hunters who excavated the site said that at ten feet of depth, they uncovered a copper chest. The shovel made a hole in the chest, revealing gold bullion and coins inside, but the chest sank and disappeared in quicksand. From on top of the copper chest, before it sank, a small box of jewels was supposedly retrieved. After the treasure hunters left, an old man who claimed to have witnessed the digging stayed in the area and convinced people from Dayton to resume digging. Their bulldozer found bones, pottery and other artifacts, but no treasure. A 1957 excavation used a dragline in the Money Hole. Flooding from the Trinity River caused Bowie Creek to flood the site, which ended the excavation. This story is a lot like the "Big Thicket Cache" story in Liberty County.

LIMESTONE COUNTY

Hightower Cache

In the 1800s, John Hightower had a ranch near Bremond, Robertson County, but lived at Kosse. He was rumored to have hidden his fortune near his house in a ravine. He died about 1920. This cache could be in Falls County.

Marion Graham Treasure

Bootlegger-rancher Marion Graham died of a heart attack in the 1930s. About $300,000 was missing from his estate. Searches on his ranch near Kosse resulted in only one small cache being recovered. In the past, his son stood guard while his father deposited money somewhere close to a plum thicket near his ranch headquarters.

LIVE OAK COUNTY

Bandit Lake Loot

See Nueces County.

Carmel Place Treasure

Near Lagarto, gold coins were reportedly buried at the Carmel Place.

Chest of Gold

A treasure chest of gold coins was said to have been buried on the west bank of the Nueces River where El Camino Real from Laredo to Goliad crossed the river. This was said to have been at Puente de Piedra.

Fort Merrill Treasures

Close to a large oak tree near Fort Merrill, two burro loads of gold bars worth $100,000 were supposedly buried during an Indian attack. Located about three miles northwest of Dinero and southeast of George West, Fort Merrill was called Little Fort or El Fortin in its short life from 1853 to 1855. The Mikeska community was near Fort Merrill. Fort Merrill was on the west side of the Nueces River. In the area, Comanches reportedly captured a locked iron safe with Spanish treasure inside. They dragged the safe into the brush but could not open it. They abandoned it. Another treasure was said to have been hidden below Fort Merrill, near Paso Valeno on the Nueces River.

Fort Ramirez Caches

J. Frank Dobie wrote about the Fort Ramirez caches, as Fort Ramirez was on his father's cattle ranch. He was familiar with the site and its legends. A gold coins treasure was said to be hidden near Fort Ramirez on Ramirez Creek. Fort Ramirez was known as the Ojo de Agua Ramirena Rancho and was a fortified sheep ranch. A wagon's supplies were rumored to have been cached near the Ramirena watering place between Casa Blanca and the Ramirena Ranch. Over the years, treasure hunters have dug extensively in the old fort and destroyed the ruins.

Jesse James Three Rivers Loot

Jesse James's gold coins loot (or part of Hernando Cortez's treasure that was discovered by Jesse James) was rumored to be hidden near Three Rivers close to where the Frio River, Nueces River and Atascosa River meet. This tale seems to be based in part on Jesse Lee James III's book *Jesse James and the Lost Cause*, which also claimed Robert Ford did not murder Jesse James on April 3, 1882.

Mexican Stash

Gold and silver bars were said to have been cached near Lake Corpus Christi. This stash could be in Trinity County.

Nueces Flats Cache

See Bee County.

Oakville Outlaws Caches

In 1876, Texas Rangers reportedly raided the outlaw town of Oakville. Outlaws were rumored to have left caches in the area.

Padres Nueces Treasure

Near the Nueces River below Lagarto, Spanish padres supposedly cached treasure during an Indian attack.

Rock Pens Treasure

See McMullen County.

San Casimore Cache

A silver and gold cache was rumored to be located in the Three Rivers area.

LLANO COUNTY

Chief Yellow Wolf's Lost Mine

Comanche chief Yellow Wolf's Lost Mine was rumored to be near the Llano River and Colorado River junction or where the North Llano River and South Llano River meet. Near London and old San Saba Presidio was another rumored location of Chief Yellow Wolf's lost silver mine. In 1851, Chief Yellow Wolf had a white settler hammer some silver ore from this mine into ornaments. This legend in *Coronado's Children* indicated it was three suns' travel west, which covers a lot of ground and many counties. In 1854, Chief Yellow Wolf was killed. Kimble County and Williamson County are other rumored locations.

The Llano River was a marker for several treasures and lost mines. *Library of Congress.*

Gold Outcrop

Not far from Austin along the Llano River, a sample of an outcrop was said to have had an assay value of $12,000 of gold per ton. It could be in Burnet County.

Harp Perry Mine and Treasure

See San Saba County.

Jim Bowie's Lost Silver Mines

See Menard County.

Little Llano Lost Mine and Treasure

A lost mine with gold and silver ore was rumored to be near the Little Llano River. Also near the Little Llano River, an old smelter site was said to mark the site of a half-million dollars in gold and silver coins. This could be in Menard County, Schleicher County or Sutton County.

Los Mina de las Almagres Mining District/Lost San Saba Mine/ Lost Almagres Mine/Lost Amarillas Mine

Los Mina de las Almagres was a Spanish Texas mining district. A group of Spanish prospectors under Don Bernardo de Miranda y Flores departed San Antonio in February 1756 to investigate silver deposit locations related by Apache Indians. Stories about a number of lost mines were told about this area. Miranda's party claimed to have found silver ore embedded in Cerro del Almagre, a reddish hill (probably due to iron). Three pounds of ore samples caused more mineral expeditions to investigate other stories of Indian silver mines in the area. There were a number of Spanish mines, but the mines may not have been profitable and were under Indian attacks. See Harry Sinclair Drago's *Lost Bonanzas* and David C. Lewis's *The San Saba Treasure: Legends of Silver Creek* for more information. This could be in Mason County, McCulloch County and/or San Saba County. See chapter 3, "Lost Mines."

Lost Blanco Mine

The Spanish Lost Blanco Mine was reportedly on Packsaddle Mountain (a different Packsaddle Mountain is in Brewster County) near the Colorado River and Llano River junction about five miles southwest of Kingsland, with its entrance hidden under a flat stone. A man named Blanco was said to have rediscovered the old mine; however, the name Blanco probably came from the Blanco River, which flows through white (*blanco*) limestone in the area. Larimore also found the mine and did mining before hiding the entrance and leaving the country. Roland claimed to have found the mine and worked to sell it for $1,000, but the deal was never finalized. Wyatt was said to have found a silver nugget on an animal skin in a cave in the area. An old Spanish colonial period mine southwest of the Llano River near Honey Creek was documented in guidebook 20 of the Austin Geological Society's *Geology and Historical Mining, Llano Uplift Region, Central Texas* as well as in a master's thesis by Nancy Ellen Mayo. This mine was likely mined out and could have been the Lost Blanco Mine.

Lost Iguanas Mine/Lost Mina de las Iguanas

See Menard County.

Lost Mathews Mine

This mine was supposed to be near Castell. It could be in Mason County.

Outlaw Llano Cave Loot

Outlaw loot was rumored to be buried in a cave near Llano.

Rangers Treasure

McCulloch's Texas Rangers were chasing Indians through a narrow valley along a stream when one of the rangers reportedly saw gold nuggets while getting a drink in the stream. Some think the rangers were northwest of Oxford. The rangers collected gold nuggets and, on the top of a low hill, found a forked tree with an old rusty pickax with a rotted handle pointing to the stream head. No one reported finding the source of the nuggets.

Rube Bouce Loot

Rube Bouce reportedly hid his loot near his home near Llano.

Sam Bass Trinity River Loot

Sam Bass reportedly hid $60,000 in coins near Castell near the Mason County boundary on the south side of the Trinity River. Another story was that Sam Bass or some other outlaw hid loot in a cave on Packsaddle Mountain. A Mexican worker putting up fences on Packsaddle Mountain was said to have found the cave, taken the loot and left behind a mail sack with "U.S." written on it. Others say the treasure was never found. It could be in Mason County.

Spanish Kingsland Treasure

Near Kingsland, a Spanish treasure of silver bullion and church treasure worth $3 million was reportedly cached.

William Nard Lost Mine

This lost silver or lead mine was said to have been near Sandy Creek and Cedar Mountain. William or Bill Nard was a bee hunter who carried a sack with him. Sometimes it was filled with ore. He supplied the people of this area with lead for their bullets. In the late 1860s, he died without showing anyone the location of his lead mine.

LOVING COUNTY

Montezuma Pecos Treasure.

See Reeves County

Pecos River La Mina Perdida (The Lost Mine)/Lost Perdida Mine

See Reeves County.

MARION COUNTY

Lost Caddo Lead Mine

See Harrison County.

MARTIN COUNTY

Cistern Loot

A legend indicated outlaws robbed a Texas Pacific train near Stanton. A posse quickly caught them. Most of the loot was not on the outlaws, indicating they stashed it. It was thought they dropped it in a cistern on the edge of Stanton while they were being chased. Could also be in Howard County, Midland County or Reagan County.

Tarzan Treasures

Several miles southwest of Tarzan, a rich man was rumored to have buried his wealth before dying, and it was not found. Another story claimed two men (one man) found a trunk in river sands close to Tarzan. Before the trunk could be recovered, water covered it and buried it under sand and clay. Frank, one of the two men (or brothers) came to Tarzan about 1955 and searched a creek area about 2.5 miles southwest of Tarzan for the treasure.

MASON COUNTY

Harp Perry Mine and Treasure

See San Saba County.

Jim Bowie's Lost Silver Mines

See Menard County.

John W. Gamel Cache

Rich rancher John W. Gamel lived on the edge of Mason, which was the beginning of the Dodge Cattle Trail. He drove cattle to market and let his wife, Kate, hide their silver coins cache. One day in 1870, he found Kate dead in the potato cellar after he returned from a trip. In spite of much digging and searching, John W. Gamel never found his hidden fortune.

Los Mina de las Almagres Mining District/Lost San Saba Mine/ Lost Almagres Mine/Lost Amarillas Mine

See Llano County.

Lost Mathews Mine

See Llano County.

Reese Butler Mine

Blacksmith Reese Butler of San Marcos saved an Indian's life. The Indian repaid him by showing him a gold and silver deposit. Once a year, Butler supposedly left San Marcos in his wagon and returned a month later with valuable ore. At his blacksmith furnace, Butler refined the ore into silver bars. He sold his silver to Austin jewelers. His silver mine was said to have been on the Llano River, maybe near where Threadgill Creek (may be called something else now) joined it.

Sam Bass Trinity River Loot

See Llano County.

MATAGORDA COUNTY

Constitution

See Calhoun County.

Independence

See Calhoun County.

Lafitte Colorado River Treasures

Pirate Jean Lafitte reportedly buried treasure overlooking Gold Point up the Colorado River. Another tale was that a Spanish warship blocked the mouth of the Colorado River and kept a pirate ship from escaping. The pirates buried their treasure chest. This treasure chest was reportedly later recovered by treasure hunters.

Lafitte Treasure Found

Dr. Joseph S. Wooten found an old parchment in a cave in the Rio Grande area in 1910. It was in French and had an *X* marking a Jean Lafitte treasure location on the Gulf of Mexico. Joni Benuit, who was said to be one of Jean Lafitte's men, had signed the parchment. With two other men, Dr. Wooten followed the map to Matagorda Island and dug up two chests with $86,000 in gold and silver coins, low-value jewels and other items.

Meteor

See Calhoun County.

Palmetto

See Calhoun County.

Santa Rosa

See Calhoun County.

MAVERICK COUNTY

Cassidy's Gold

Cassidy buried his gold somewhere between Frio Town, Frio County and Eagle Pass, Maverick County, before he was killed by bandits. It could be in Frio County or Zavala County.

Jesse James Eagle Pass Treasure

Near Eagle Pass, Jesse James was said to have cached gold coins. Another legend indicated Jesse James and Quantrill stole an Aztec treasure in Mexico and hid it possibly near Eagle Pass along the Rio Grande.

McNeal Brothers Silver Coins

The two McNeal brothers from the Brazos River area traded goods in Eagle Pass for silver and gold coins. After some dispute at Eagle Pass, they headed home with their coins and were followed by Mexican soldiers. Deciding to hide their coins, they noticed drying cracks in the hard soil. They reportedly unpacked the coins from their bags and carefully dropped them into the cracks. They covered the cracks with dry dirt. The Mexican soldiers caught up with them and let them go, since they had no money on them. The two brothers backtracked to the cache site, but the cracks in the hard soil were deep, so they needed shovels and picks to dig up their coins. They set up markers and left. By the time they returned, floods had washed their markers away. The once-dry cracks containing the coins were filled in with soil deposits, so they couldn't locate them.

McCULLOCH COUNTY

Harp Perry Mine and Treasure

See San Saba County.

Lead Balls Treasure

See Menard County.

Los Mina de las Almagres Mining District/Lost San Saba Mine/ Lost Almagres Mine/Lost Amarillas Mine

See Llano County.

Lost Spanish Calf Creek Mine

A Spanish mine was said to have been on Calf Creek near the town of Calf Creek. Spaniards abandoned their mine when Comanches attacked and stole their horses. A map showing its location was in the hands of a Mexican family over the years.

Onion Creek Gold

Gold bullion may have been buried north of Brady on Onion Creek.

McLENNAN COUNTY

Crawford Caches

On the William Tubbs Farm about four miles north of Crawford, $1,000 to $1,500 in gold coins was recovered. On Captain Bewley's farm, $6,800 was found in several places. The money may have come from Tonkawa Indians who lived near present-day Crawford on a reservation. About 1859, the Tonkawas were paid $40,000 in gold before they left the area. More gold coins may remain there.

Gambling Gold

A man reportedly won $1,200 in a craps game near the Waco stockyards and hid it based on the location of several cotton bales. The cotton bales were moved, so he could not locate his cache.

McMullen County

Las Chuzas Mine and Treasure

Near Las Chuzas Mountains and Caja Mountain, Indians once reportedly operated a silver mine. Spanish or Mexican miners came and had silver bars cached in the mine (or a low spot) before the mine entrance was hidden with rocks. A similar legend has a Mexican or Spanish treasure of gold and silver bullion hidden in a cave near the San Cajas Mountains or San Cajo Mountain when Indians attacked between the Las Chuzas mine and Nueces River. The few who survived fled to Mexico—never returning. This could be in La Salle County.

Lost Estambel Hill Treasures

See La Salle County.

Nueces River Treasure Found

One story in *Legends of Texas* volume 1 told of several Mexicans looking for a hidden treasure at the Nueces River crossing on the San Antonio–Laredo Road. The treasure was General Cos's Mexican army payroll. Upon hearing of Santa Anna's defeat, Mexican soldiers dug a hole, buried the payroll and burned a wagon over it. Years later, a group of Mexicans looking for the treasure reportedly found a freshly dug empty hole with coin indentations in the dirt. They were a week or so too late. Someone else got the treasure.

Rock Arrow Treasure

Indians supposedly attacked a Mexican party moving treasure. The legend indicated that the Mexicans buried their treasure on the southeast side of Alta Loma Mountain. To mark the cache, they lined up rocks to form an arrow pointing to the site. Cattle grazing over the years may have moved the rocks and destroyed the arrow.

Rock Pens Treasure

Dan Dunham belonged to an outlaw gang that raided northern Mexico. Indians attacked the gang in a ravine where Dunham's gang had constructed a rock pen for their campsite and a rock pen for their mules and horses. Dunham's companions were killed. Dunham was wounded and escaped to a nearby fort—possibly Fort Ewell. Another version of this story has Dunham leaving to get help while his men held off the Indians. Dunham died in 1873, leaving guidance to the fort's doctor for a $5–$6 million treasure of gold and silver (thirty or thirty-one mule loads). Reportedly the treasure was six or seven miles below the Laredo Crossing on the south side of the Nueces River near the hills. Some believed it was at a Nueces River crossing on the Shiner Ranch. The rock pens were said to have been located east of a small spring coming out from under a rock. Many have searched the area, and a few claimed to have found the pens before learning about the lost treasure. Another version has the men being miners rather than outlaws. This could be in Duval County, Jim Hogg County, La Salle County or Live Oak County.

San Caja Mountains Treasures

In the San Cajo (Caja) Mountains, a legend indicated Spaniards (miners or outlaws) got lost traveling from Mexico to San Antonio with two cowhide bags of gold doubloons and ran out of water. When their burros died, they cached the gold in a rock crevice covered with a flat rock with a cross carved on it. Everyone in the party later died.

Another version of this legend was that Mexicans with nine burro loads of silver bullion from northern Mexico mines buried the silver to save their burros and themselves after running out of water. A variation of this legend claimed the Mexicans were outlaws who hid Spanish dollars, gold candlesticks and other loot in a San Cajo Mountains cave between San Antonio and Laredo. Probably the same story in part as McMullen County, "Las Chuzas Mine and Treasure." This could be in La Salle County.

Seven Rocks Hill Silver

A Mexico-bound party with seven mule loads of silver ($350,000 in silver bullion) were in the Seven Rocks Hill or Loma de Siete Piedras area when Indians attacked them. One legend claimed the Mexicans cached the silver. Another version has Indians hiding it. This was said to be near Fowlerton or Seven Rocks. It could be in La Salle County.

Train Robbery Loot

See Terrell County.

MEDINA COUNTY

Lost Estambel Hill Treasures

See La Salle County.

Horse Trader's Cache

See Bexar County.

MENARD COUNTY

Buck Creek Treasures

See San Saba County.

Bullion Cache

See Kimble County.

Jack Wilkinson Treasure

In 1872, W.J. "Jack" Wilkinson was said to have buried a half-gallon jar full of $10,000 in gold coins near a corral on his ranch before he and Watt Key drove their cattle to New Orleans. While he was away, Mrs. Key stayed with Mrs. Wilkinson, as Mrs. Wilkinson was pregnant. Hogs rooting in the log smokehouse uncovered the $10,000 in gold coins. Mrs. Wilkinson reburied the treasure near their corrals on the San Saba River in what is known as Wilkinson's Hole. Mrs. Wilkinson suddenly died in premature childbirth a few days later. Her husband and others never found the treasure. The ranch house was on the north side of the San Saba River north of Hext. Another version of this story was that a horse thief buried the treasure on the Wilkinson Ranch.

Jim Bowie's Lost Silver Mines

Adventurer Jim Bowie and his brother looked for lost Spanish mines near San Saba Presidio and were rumored to have found some. *Library of Congress.*

Jim Bowie commanded several expeditions in search of lost silver mines in the San Saba River and Llano River region. According to some legends, he found the mines, but other stories insist he found no mines. In 1831, Jim Bowie led his first party of nine prospectors looking for the Lost Almagres Mine in the San Saba-Llano country with the permission of the Mexican government. Bowie's party encountered an Indian war party on November 2, 1831, and was forced to fight for their lives at either Calf Creek (east of San Saba Presidio) or Silver Creek (west of San Saba Presidio). One of Bowie's men was killed and, reportedly, forty Indians were killed and thirty Indians wounded. Bowie and his men returned to San Antonio in December 1831 and left with a bigger force to search for lost mines.

Near the town of San Saba, a Lost Bowie Mine was supposedly situated. A legend indicated Spanish soldiers worked the mine before Indians attacked them. Silver worth $33 million was rumored to be hidden before the mine was blown up by gunpowder. Most of these Spaniards died on their way to Mexico. The survivors didn't return to the mine. One story claimed Jim Bowie and twenty miners used the site of the Mission San Saba and San Saba Presidio as their base camp and recovered much silver from nearby mines.

Another tale indicated Jim Bowie stashed about $25 million in silver bars along the San Saba River north of Menard. Silver Creek, located just west of San Saba Presidio, had mining over the years. One version has Jim Bowie's brother Rezin Bowie finding the mine and getting ore samples, which were rich. Some claim Jim Bowie got his silver from raiding Mexican mule trains. Harry Sinclair Drago's *Lost Bonanzas* has a good account of this legend. Jim Bowie died at the Alamo, but his brother became a planter and Louisiana politician. This could be in Llano County, Mason County, McCulloch County and/or San Saba County.

Lead Balls Treasure

Spaniards near an old mine near San Saba Presidio were said to have laid out four lead balls filled with gold nuggets to form a square 411 yards apart. In the early 1900s, one of the lead balls was found. This could be in McCulloch County or San Saba County.

Little Llano Lost Mine and Treasure

See Llano County.

Lost Iguanas Mine/Lost Mina de las Iguanas

A legend indicated the Lost Iguanas Mine with two thousand or seven thousand 50-pound silver bars was near the northwest forks of the San Saba River and Silver Creek. This may be in Llano County or San Saba County.

Mission San Saba Treasure

On the San Saba River near Mission San Saba (Mission Santa Cruz de San Saba), gold and silver bars were supposedly stashed in a mine shaft. Remains of an old smelter were discovered at the site, which indicated mining in the

The San Saba River flows through the area of the legendary Lost San Saba Mine and other lost mines. *Author.*

area. In spite of extensive digging at the mission over the years, no treasure has been found. Archaeologists have investigated the mission site.

Pegleg Crossing Loot

Loot ($30,000 in gold coins) from an 1883 robbery was rumored hidden near Pegleg Crossing of the San Saba River, about twelve miles southeast of Menard at McDougal Creek near State Highway 29. Robbers Roost. where robberies occurred, is one mile west of Pegleg Crossing. Another tale has Jim Bowie robbing a Mexican wagon train with twenty tons of silver en route to Mexico. Jim Bowie was said to have hidden the silver at Pegleg Crossing.

MIDLAND COUNTY

Cave Gold

See Upton County.

Cistern Loot

See Martin County.

MILAM COUNTY

Mission San Gabriel Treasure

Mission San Gabriel's treasure of nine mule loads of gold heading for Mexico was supposedly cached on the San Gabriel River near Thorndale. Another version of this legend indicated the treasure was $1 million in gold coins. A man called Snively reportedly was killed and buried with the treasure so his ghost would guard it. Another version has a priest murdered and buried to guard the gold.

William Nard Lost Mine

See Llano County.

MILLS COUNTY

Cow Pens Gold Coins

See San Saba County.

Mose Jackson Treasure

In 1850, Mose Jackson was rumored to have hidden a fruit jar of gold coins in the Rattler Community near a spring, maybe a few hundred yards from his house. On Pecan Bayou, raiding Indians murdered Mose Jackson and his wife while they gathered pecans. The Indians captured Mose Jackson's children. Texas Rangers rescued the children, who did not know where their parents hid the money. It could be in Brown County.

Sam Williams Cache

Sam Williams was said to have cached $4,000 in gold coins in a quart-sized can near Mullin in 1880, close to the Sims Place. Williams rode with Quantrill during the Civil War and had a past. He told his wife he had buried money, but not where. Soon afterward, he was ambushed and killed while tending his horses.

San Saba Junction Treasure

See San Saba County.

Spanish Treasure Boxes

Spanish padres reportedly had four copper boxes with part of a map in each box showing where treasure from New Mexico and Colorado mines was hidden in a cave or old mine. An iron spike in a pecan tree was a marker to the treasure. Three copper boxes were buried. A man acquired the fourth copper box and the location of the three buried boxes. About 1900, near Epley Springs, which is northeast of Goldthwaite, Dr. James Kirkpatrick learned about this lost treasure from a stranger. Dr. Kirkpatrick found a woodcutter who had cut down a tree with an iron spike in it. The woodcutter showed Dr. Kirkpatrick the old tree with the spike. Dr. Kirkpatrick recovered a buried copper box containing a gold cross with pearls and two ivory and rosewood rosaries. The name Padre Lopez and a 1762 date were on the box. Dr. Kirkpatrick also found a flat rock with symbols. He deciphered it as saying fifteen mule loads of gold and silver were hidden in a cave also. Dr. Kirkpatrick and the landowner of the place where he believed the treasure was located never came to terms. In 1904, Dr. Kirkpatrick died. His wife reportedly took the rock with symbols to California. Another treasure hunter later reportedly found another copper box. Steve Wilson's *True Treasure* article "Cryptic Copper Plates—Clues to a Spanish Treasure?" has a lot of information on this tale.

MITCHELL COUNTY

Chief Lone Wolf Treasure

On Lone Wolf Mountain, Kiowa chief Lone Wolf was said to have been buried with treasure in 1879.

MONTAGUE COUNTY

Lost Spanish Fort Gold Mine

About thirty miles north of Bowie, legends indicated there was a lost Spanish Fort gold mine. A French settlement and abandoned mining were nearby. This area has sedimentary rock on the surface, so a lost gold mine is not likely.

Sam Bass Bowie Loot

Near Bowie, northwest of Denton, Sam Bass was said to have hidden $30,000 in gold coins. It was supposedly buried below a forked tree.

Spanish Fort Loot Found

Outlaw brothers were suspected of hiding loot near their hideout in the Nacona and Spanish Fort area in the 1870s. The brothers were reportedly captured after stealing some horses in Denton County and hanged. H.L. Alley reported in a July 1967 article in the *Artifact* that, using a metal detector, he and a partner recovered a metal box near where the outlaw brothers' hideout

Loot from a number of stagecoach robberies was said to have been hidden in several Texas areas. *Library of Congress.*

once stood. Inside the metal box were gold and silver coins, but Alley did not report how much was found. A photo of their find showed a number of coins.

Spanish Fort Treasure

An old Mexican map reportedly indicated a treasure buried near a tree and bluff close to where the Red River headed south. One legend said it was on the Texas side of the Red River west of Dexter, near Walnut Bend. Other stories claimed it was hidden on the Oklahoma side of Sivell's Bend. The treasure belonged to a Spanish expedition attacked by Indians; the Spaniards died. *See* Cooke County, "Walnut Bend Treasures."

Twenty or Twenty-One Jack Loads of Silver

Near Spanish Fort twenty or twenty-one mule loads of silver were reportedly thrown into a lake by Spanish or French travelers. The lake has now disappeared. Another variation of this legend has the silver hidden in a creek two miles southeast of the old fort. A version was that at the Illinois Bend of the Red River, a Mexican (four Americans and six Mexicans) wagon train or a wagon was moving gold coins or bullion from Mexico to St. Louis. Bandits or Comanches attacked, so they supposedly buried the treasure. The lone survivor, Gonzales, escaped to Mexico and never returned. He gave directions to the treasure, but no one found it. The Spanish Trail connected Santa Fe, New Mexico, and Louisiana's Mississippi River by following the Red River.

MOORE COUNTY

Lost Pot of Gold Coins

See Hutchinson County.

MORRIS COUNTY

Mexican Agents Treasure

See Upshur County.

NACOGDOCHES COUNTY

Appleby Area Cache

Northeast of Appleby, some $75,000 worth of gold was supposedly hidden by Mexicans on the old Greening Place. One version has it hidden in an old mine shaft.

Mexican Attoyac Bayou Cache

Near Attoyac Bayou (River), a Mexican reportedly cached gold coins. This could be in Shelby County or Rusk County.

Supply Cache

In 1819, weapons and other supplies reportedly were hidden in a dry well in Nacogdoches during a revolt. This cache could be near Camp Freeman.

Wagon Loads of Gold

See San Augustine County.

NAVARRO COUNTY

Ingram's Caches

Washington Ingram was a rich famer and rancher in an area called Rural Shade on the Trinity River east of Corsicana. He settled in the area around 1850 and was said to have buried three money caches close to his ranch headquarters near the Trinity River's Wildcat Crossing. He didn't tell his family where he hid the caches. After he died at age ninety, his family searched and uncovered one cache but reportedly never found the other two caches.

Stagecoach Loot

During the 1860s, a legend claimed there was a robbery of fourteen boxes of silver and gold heading from New Orleans for San Antonio. The loot reportedly was hidden in a cave on Wolf Creek not far from Frost and Blooming Grove. Joe White's Cave and the area around it was extensively searched by a landowner's daughter and Joe White, without any reported success.

NEWTON COUNTY

Lost Lead Mines

See Jasper County and Sabine County, "Lost Lead Mines."

NOLAN COUNTY

Found Gold in Cave

An oil field hand in Sweetwater was said to have found a cave southeast of Sweetwater three miles from a road on private property. The oil field hand made multiple trips on foot there over time and recovered a number of metal bars, which contained gold as well as other metal poured in crude molds. The weight of the bars was up to about twenty pounds each. Several people saw the bars he sold. The cave was square, so it was man-made, with a door walled up with rock. The third time the oil field hand returned, he found the entrance covered with caved-in rock that he could not remove without equipment.

Nueces County

Bandit Lake Loot

Bandits who stole treasure in Mexico were rumored to have hidden it near present-day Lake Corpus Christi before they were killed or captured. In 1959, "Sourdough" Lassiter was allowed to hunt for it by the City of Corpus Christi. He never found any treasure. It could be in Live Oak County.

Fogg Treasure

John "Old Man" Fogg was said to have hidden $30,000 in cash near Corpus Christi from selling property. He lived on Chaparral Street. When he died, his cash was not accounted for.

Fort Planticlan Treasures

Near Fort Planticlan not far from Driscoll about fifteen miles below Casa Blanca, silver bars worth $1.5 million were reportedly cached. During an Indian attack, the Spaniards at Fort Planticlan reportedly buried three mule loads of silver bars. All the Spaniards were killed by the Indians but one, who told this story. In the 1920s, three Mexicans came to the area with a map, looking for the treasure. See Jim Wells County, "Casa Blanca Treasures."

Forty Mule Loads of Treasure

At the mouth of the Nueces River, forty mule loads of treasure were supposedly buried during an Indian attack. Another variation of this tale was that it was a chest with gold and other riches. A boy survived the Indian attack to tell this story. One possible site was the Riverside Ranch. This could be in San Patricio County.

Gray Treasure

Mayberry "Mustang" Gray and Billy Richards killed some Mexicans in a fight between the Rio Grande and Goliad and took their $16,000 ($6,000) in gold. Gray supposedly buried it in the Nueces River area near Paso Piedra (Rock Crossing) and never recovered it. It could be in San Patricio County.

Lafitte Mustang Island and Flour Bluff Treasures

On Mustang Island and at Flour Bluff, the pirate Jean Lafitte was rumored to have buried treasure.

Lafitte Pirate Booty

At the mouth of the Nueces River close to Corpus Christi, near a tree with an old chain around it or a spike in the ground, the pirate Jean Lafitte or other pirates reportedly hid booty.

Lost Santa Anna San Patricio Treasure Chest

One of General Santa Anna's pay chests was reportedly hidden in the Nueces River area near Paso Piedra (Rock Crossing) some three miles below San Patricio. During high water, the pay chest fell from a wagon. Several variations of this story were that it was not recovered, that it was recovered and buried under an elm tree, and that a chain was placed around the chest and fixed to a tree for later recovery. There was also a version of the story that the soldiers stole the pay chest and made up the story of it being lost. It could be in San Patricio County.

Lost Villareal Silver Mine

See San Patricio County.

Maximilian's Treasure

Another site of Maximilian's treasure ($15 million) was said to be at Flour Bluff. In 1940, Humble Oil & Gas was dredging Laguna Madre off Flour Bluff when it recovered seventy coins, mostly Maximilian-period Mexican silver dollars as well as human bones. Some coins were dated 1867. This was rumored to be part of Maximilian's hoard. John S. Potter Jr.'s story in *The Treasure Diver's Guide* (based on Dee Woods and Florence E. Shaner's book, *Blaze of Gold*) was that two Austrians survived the ex-Confederates' attack at Castle Gap. These two Austrians gathered more help and returned to Castle Gap, where they recovered the treasure and took it to Corpus Christi Bay. After the treasure was put on a boat, a storm sank the boat. What was found during 1940 dredging was rumored to be part of this treasure. *See* Upton County, "Castle Gap Treasures/Maximilian Treasure."

Money Hill Treasure

Mustang Island was rumored to have a treasure on Money Hill, which was the tallest sand dune on the island. The dunes shift over time. The highest dune was also called Big Hill or Three Mile Hill, as it was three miles south of Aransas Pass. One legend had pirates hiding money on Money Hill. It has been said coins were recovered in the area. Maybe the main treasure has been found.

Oppencoffer Treasure

Fred Oppencoffer's gold and silver coins may have been hidden on Shamrock Island, just west of Mustang Island. He died in 1917 and was rumored to have been Russian nobility and received money from his family in Russia.

Pancho Villa Treasures

On her deathbed in 1956, Delores Agilero Vasquez claimed Pancho Villa buried five treasures worth $1.5 million in the United States, including one about three to four miles from Robstown in a gully near a slaughterhouse. Another cache was supposed to be under a certain headstone in Corpus Christi. *See* Bexar County, "Pancho Villa Treasures"; Kleberg County, "Cinenia Caches/Pancho Villa Treasures"; and Starr County, "Pancho Villa Treasure."

Spanish Oso Creek Treasure

On Oso Creek near Corpus Christi, a Spanish treasure was possibly buried. It could be in San Patricio County.

Tontino's Chest

Near Corpus Christi, a man named Tontino reportedly buried a treasure chest.

Zieglar Treasure

Near Corpus Christi, in the North Beach area, Jacob Zieglar was rumored to have hidden $50,000 to $60,000. He did not use banks. When he died, his wife and others searched for his missing wealth.

OLDHAM COUNTY

Tascosa Treasures

Near Tascosa close to the Canadian River, $75,000 in gold coins (gold bullion) was said to have been cached. Another treasure of one thousand $20 gold coins was rumored to be near Tierra Draw and Frio Draw near Tascosa and the Canadian River. These two legends could be variations of the same legend. This treasure could be in Randall County.

Traders' Alamoso Creek Cache

A trading party carrying $10,000 was said to have been attacked by Indians. The traders buried their money between Alamocito Creek and Middle Alamoso Creek near the south side of the Canadian River. Two traders were killed, and the remaining ten traders fled in several groups. Only five traders made it to the Arkansas River. None were reported to have returned to recover their money.

ORANGE COUNTY

Lafitte Neches River Treasure

See Jefferson County.

Lafitte Sabine River Cache

On the Sabine River, pirate Jean Lafitte's treasure was supposedly cached.

PALO PINTO COUNTY

M.L. Dalton's Treasure

Rancher M.L. Dalton reportedly buried $20,000 to $25,000 in gold and silver coins near his ranch. He was said to have driven cattle to Kansas City and received $44,000 in gold coins for them. Indians killed Dalton in 1867. A man-made lake covers the ranch and possibly the treasure.

Panola County

Gold Treasure

See Rusk County.

Lafitte Hendricks Lake Treasure

See Rusk County.

Parker County

Found Bass Gang Gold Coins

Near Springtown, another Sam Bass treasure of gold and silver coins in a box was supposedly hidden in the Skeen's Peak area. Near Springtown, about 1900, Henry Chapman had a small farm. While in the woods between Salt Creek and Clear Fork Creek, he noticed a small mound. He dug into the mound and found a wooden box full of uncirculated 1877 gold coins like the Bass Gang stole in the Big Springs, Nebraska, train robbery. In another version of the tale, Henry Chapman claimed to have found the treasure but was scared off by horsemen he thought were outlaws. *See* Denton County, "Sam Bass Denton Treasures."

Weatherford Outlaw Loot

Near Weatherford in the 1840s, outlaws were rumored to have cached loot from numerous robberies in the Fort Worth region. All the gang members were killed by Texans, except their leader, who escaped and buried their loot. The outlaw leader stayed with a family in the area and got very ill. Before he died, he drew a map to the treasure. The husband who got the map was killed in a gunfight, so his wife gave the map to Mr. Curtis. Curtis spent many years digging in the area. Some said he found the lost loot, but others said he never found it. The loot may be near the old Curtis diggings or an old Civilian Conservation Corps (CCC) camp at the edge of Weatherford. During the Depression, boys from this CCC camp spent part of their spare time digging for the lost outlaw loot.

William Riddle Cache

See Tarrant County.

PECOS COUNTY

James Gang Ranch Treasure

Outlaws Jesse and Frank James may have had a ranch near the old Pontoon Crossing on the Pecos River about thirty miles northwest of Sheffield. They were said to have buried loot there. It could be in Crockett County.

La Mina Perdida (The Lost Mine)

A lost gold or silver mine was said in a legend to be up a canyon.

Outlaws Frank and Jesse James (pictured) had Texas hideouts and may have cached some of their loot nearby. *Library of Congress.*

Seven Mile Mountain Spanish Treasure

Indians reportedly attacked Spanish conquistadores with treasure and other goods northeast of current Fort Stockton. The conquistadores hid their treasure and were all killed. A leather pouch with eight pounds of gold nuggets and a skeleton have been found in the area.

Shephard Brothers Loot

Clell and Oliver Shephard were said to have robbed a wagon train of fifteen chests of gold bars, which they stashed in a cave. This could have been Emperor Maximilian's Treasure at Castle Gap. Over the years, they only took enough to live on. In 1887, both died in an accident, so the remaining loot is still cached. *See* Upton County, "Castle Gap Treasures/Maximilian Treasure."

Train Robbery Loot

See Terrell County.

Two Cannons

Several brass cannons were reportedly hidden near Horsehead Crossing. They could be in Crane County.

Polk County

Bad Luck Creek Lost Gold Coins

Around 1868 or 1869, a man with three hundred or five hundred gold coins worth about $50,000 was said to have become lost on Bad Luck Creek while en route on foot to buy land from Eli Hall. He left White Oak Settlement (now Thicket) and became lost along a winding creek. On his eighth day of wandering, he hid the gold in a creek bank under a holly tree that partially hid the hole. He reached civilization but was unable to find the location of his gold coins later.

Bad Luck Creek may have gotten its name due to this man losing his gold there. Another story was that a settler got shot there during a fight between other parties and the creek was named after his bad luck of being in the wrong place at the wrong time. This treasure could be in Hardin County.

Cannon Treasure

See Angelina County.

Presidio County

Apache Gold

Apaches were rumored to have buried a strongbox of gold in a cave on Cibalo Creek not far from Shafter, an old silver mining town.

Cariza Pass Treasure

A wealthy Mexican miner reportedly moved his $3 million fortune in gold and silver in twenty-seven carts to Texas in 1863, during the Juaristas' war against Emperor Maximilian. After crossing the Rio Grande into Texas, they camped at Cariza Pass. Bandits following the treasure train attacked their camp. The miner and his men cached the treasure during the fight. The bandits killed all the party but one. Texas Rangers arrived and saved the survivor. The survivor died in a San Antonio hospital, after telling his rescuers where the treasure was cached. A search party did not find it.

Top: Apaches were said to have hidden gold near the silver-mining town of Shafter. *Library of Congress.*

Bottom: A rancher's cattle money was said to have been cached near El Fortin de Cibolo. *Library of Congress.*

Cattle Sale Cache

A rancher was said to have cached money from the sale of his cattle in Kansas between Fort Davis and the Rio Grande near El Fortin de Cibolo. It was said outlaws followed and murdered the rancher without finding his money.

Ebony Cross Treasure

See Jeff Davis County.

La Mina Perdida Treasure

Near Marfa, gold bars were supposedly cached in La Mina Perdida. This treasure could be in Jeff Davis County.

Lost Chico Mine

In an abandoned mine, Mexican soldiers were rumored to have hidden plunder consisting of one-half ton of gold bars and other loot.

Mexican Payroll Loot

In 1924, a Mexican payroll was reportedly robbed of Mexican gold coins and U.S. currency. It may have been hidden under a house not far from Presidio.

Paisano Pass Gold

See Brewster County.

Pinto Canyon Treasure

Some 105 mule loads of treasure from Mexico were reportedly buried in Palo Pinto Canyon.

RANDALL COUNTY

Casner Treasure

Three Casner brothers and their father, John Casner, were successful California gold miners who headed east with their gold. Two of the brothers set up a sheep ranch in Texas, while the father and his other son went prospecting in California, Arizona and New Mexico. In 1876, two of the Casner brothers (J. Casner) were supposed to have buried $20,000 in $20 gold coins in Palo

Duro Canyon, from California gold minted into coins in Arizona or Carson City, Nevada. The two Casner brothers grazed a large number of sheep in the Palo Duro Canyon area and appear to have hidden most of the newly minted gold pieces in the area. They had a neighbor, Charles Goodnight, who lived in what is now Palo Duro Canyon. A bandit called Sostenes L'Archeveque murdered the two Casner brothers; he hated Americans because Americans had killed his father. Sostenes L'Archeveque reportedly killed twenty-three Americans over his lifetime. Sostenes robbed the two Casners of money but not the $20,000 or so in the newly minted coins in their hidden cache. Sostenes killed a young Indian sheepherder along with the two Casners after the sheepherder showed them where a pouch of gold was hidden. Sostenes L'Archeveque was later killed. The Casner brothers' father and other brother sought revenge and reportedly killed anyone who had $20 gold pieces similar to the minted coins the Casner brothers had. Some of those who were killed by the Casners reportedly got the money from Colas Martinez, whom the Casners also killed. The money from some of these men may have been spent by the Casner brothers for supplies, not stolen. Many think the $20,000 was possibly hidden in the area of the current Palo Duro State Park, some forty miles from Tascosa. This could be in Armstrong County.

Grachias Treasure

At the Lighthouse Canyon and Palo Duro Canyon junction, Jesus Ramon Grachias in the 1880s recovered a chest containing $7,600 ($7,000) in Spanish coins that his father had buried. Three other chests with gold and silver bars were said not to have been recovered. This treasure was supposedly part of Santa Anna's money that was hidden by Mexican soldiers after Texans defeated the Mexican army at San Jacinto.

Traders' Alamoso Creek Cache

See Oldham County.

REAGAN COUNTY

Cistern Loot

See Martin County.

REAL COUNTY

Camp Wood Spanish Treasure and Lead-Silver Mines

A legend said Spaniards buried seventeen mule loads of silver during a Comanche attack near the Nueces River. An old Spanish mine with lead and silver was reportedly near Camp Wood. Old mine shafts are found in the area. Some Spanish relics and silver-lead ore have reportedly been found near Mission San Lorenzo and Camp Wood. Near the town of Leakey, Indians and Mexicans supposedly had a lead and silver mine. This could be in Uvalde County.

Lost Silver Ledge

A silver ledge was said to be near the Frio River (Frio Canyon). It could be in Uvalde County.

Tom Wall Treasure

Wealthy businessman Tom Wall reportedly stashed $25,000 or more in gold in Frio Canyon before fleeing Texas in 1867 over murder charges. It could be in Uvalde County.

RED RIVER COUNTY

Rancher's Cache

Near English, which was located about six miles northwest of Avery, a rich rancher reportedly cached his coins.

REEVES COUNTY

Confederate Gold

A gold shipment from Confederates at Genoa, Nevada, was supposedly buried in the Davis Mountains near Toyahvale (Toyah) to avoid Union capture during the Civil War. It could be in Jeff Davis County.

Jose Vaca's Cave Gold

A cave containing gold was rumored to be in the Tecolote Mountains just below Pecos.

Montezuma Pecos Treasure

A legend claimed a cave near Pecos hides one of Montezuma's Aztec treasures. A large black or white rock reportedly covered the cave opening. A cross carved on a nearby rock was a marker. The site is on a Spanish trail from Pecos to Santa Fe, New Mexico. It could be in Loving County or Ward County.

Right: A number of legends said Montezuma's Aztec treasure was hidden at several places in Texas. *Wikimedia*.

Pecos River La Mina Perdida (The Lost Mine)/Lost Perdida Mine

La Mina Perdida gold mine may have been on the Pecos River. It could be in Loving County or Ward County.

REFUGIO COUNTY

El Copono Treasures

During the War of Texas Independence, a number of Mexican citizens fled from El Copono (Copano), which was a small community established around 1749, about twenty miles north of Corpus Christi on Copano Bay. Legends indicated some refugees left behind treasure they were never able to recover.

119

Jars of Gold Coins

Between Austwell and Refugio, eight jars of Mexican gold coins were rumored to have been hidden near the Bugantine (Bergantin, Brigatine) Creek headwaters.

Lost Spanish Payroll

See Aransas County.

St. Marys Treasures

Near the ghost town of St. Marys on Copano Bay near present Bayside, several treasures were said to have been hidden.

ROCKWALL COUNTY

Spanish Spring Treasure

See Dallas County.

RUSK COUNTY

Gold Treasure

About $15,000 worth of gold coins were rumored hidden near Tatum. This treasure could be in Panola County.

Lafitte Hendricks Lake Treasure

In 1816, at Matagorda Bay, Jean Lafitte and his pirates reportedly looted $2 million in silver bullion from the Spanish frigate (brig) *Santa Rosa*, which was heading to Spain. Spanish warships hunted Lafitte's ship, so the silver was placed in six wagons under Gaspar (Caspar) Trammel, who traded between Spanish Texas and the United States. Trammel's wagons were camped at Hendricks Lake when Spanish troops attacked them.

The silver bullion was said to have been dumped into Hendricks Lake near the junction of three counties on the old Trammel Trail. Hendricks Lake is an oxbow lake about one and a half miles south of Ramsdale's Crossing and Ferry on the Sabine River, about four miles northeast of present Tatum. One version of the legend indicated the silver was hidden near Martin Creek southeast of Tatum. Wagon driver Robert Dawson reportedly escaped to St. Louis. Many years later, Dawson returned to Hendricks Lake and searched for the treasure. Since the lake levels had changed over time and the land was much altered, Dawson gave up hunting for the treasure.

In 1835, Fox Tatum tried to drain the lake. In 1855 and 1884, others searched for the treasure. In 1895, a group from Mexico looked for the treasure. One story claimed the treasure was in forty feet of water under ten feet of mud. Three men fishing in 1921 or 1928 found three silver bars in Hendricks Lake. This could be in Panola County. See Calhoun County, "*Santa Rosa.*"

Mexican Attoyac Bayou Cache

See Nacogdoches County.

SABINE COUNTY

Flower Hamilton Cache

In 1858, rancher Flower Hamilton supposedly hid his fortune on his ranch near Brookeland. He owned the Asa Hickman Place. Many thought this cache was on Trout Bayou in a swampy area about one mile north of his ranch house. Some believed he buried it in the woods. One treasure hunter using marks cut on trees thought he found it one mile north on Trout Bayou when he got great signals with his metal detector. After digging down a couple of feet, water and quicksand prevented further digging. Lake Sam Rayburn now backs up water over this area. This cache could be in Angelina County.

Lost Lead Mines

A lead mine was supposedly south of Brookeland in the McKim Creek, Rock Creek and Beef Creek area. Several other lost mines were said to be in the region. It could be in Jasper County or Newton County.

SAN AUGUSTINE COUNTY

Wagon Loads of Gold

A legend indicated a Spanish wagon train carrying gold was going from San Augustine to Nacogdoches when it became aware of Texans fighting Spaniards in Nacogdoches. The gold was offloaded and hidden on the east bank of the Attoyac River north of San Augustine near present Texas Highway 21. Spanish treasure markings were said to have been found in the area. This could be in Nacogdoches County.

SAN PATRICIO COUNTY

Colonel Yell

During the Mexican War, on July 13, 1847, the American 233-ton steamship *Colonel Yell* with $65,000 in specie was stranded at Aransas Pass with no loss of life. This ship was built in 1847. It could be in Aransas County.

Forty Mule Loads of Treasure

See Nueces County.

Gray Treasure

See Nueces County.

Lost Santa Anna San Patricio Treasure Chest

See Nueces County.

Lost Villareal Silver Mine

Captain Enrique de Villareal owned Rincon del Oso and grazed cattle starting in 1810. His ranch headquarters was on McGloin's Bluff on Corpus Christi Bay. He was said to have found a silver mine two days' ride from his headquarters, which could be about twenty miles or so away. Some think it was near Edroy and White's Point on the Nueces River. His land grant later became part of the King Ranch. The silver mine was also supposedly near Corpus Christi. It could be in Nueces County or other counties.

Nueces Flats Cache

See Bee County.

Rancher's Gold

On his ranch, a blind rancher was said to have hidden gold coins.

Round Lake Treasure

Mexicans reportedly cached treasure near Mathis or near the Irish immigrant community of San Patricio.

Spanish Oso Creek Treasure

See Nueces County.

Sterling Dobie Treasure

Around 1880, Sterling Dobie died. He reportedly stashed about $50,000 or $35,000 in gold coins near a fence on his place near Mathis. Another version of the story has most of the $5,000 caches being recovered by Sterling Dobie's children. Two cans containing coins were reportedly never found. Also, $30,000 was said to be unaccounted for and thought to have been hidden.

SAN SABA COUNTY

Beasley Cave Ore

Beasley reportedly discovered and lost a cave filled with silver ore from a mine. Its location could be a few miles below where the Colorado River and San Saba River join. It may be in Lampasas County.

Buck Creek Treasures

In the 1700s, near the headwaters of Buck Creek where it junctions with the San Saba River, Spaniards were rumored to have hidden five caches totaling ten thousand silver bars and several cartloads of gold bars. One location was supposed to be about ten miles east of the city of San Saba. It may be in Menard County.

Cow Pens Gold Coins

Near some cow pens, a silver coins treasure was said to have been cached. Could also be in Brown County or Mills County, as it was said to be near their county lines.

Harp Perry Mine and Treasure

In the 1830s or earlier, Harp Perry, two assistants and thirty-five miners were supposedly mining silver in the San Saba River-Llano River area. They smelted the silver ore near the mine and sent ten to twelve burros laden with silver to San Antonio from time to time. Perry reportedly buried about 1,500 pounds of silver near the mine and smelter for safe keeping. In 1834, a Comanche Indian raid killed all but Harp Perry, several men and a Mexican girl (or only Perry and another American survived). Perry didn't return to the area until 1865. The area had changed, so he could not find the markers to his buried silver. He was said to have offered $500 for someone to lead him to an old smelter near a spring. His treasure was supposedly hidden about one-half mile due north of the spring. A pin oak tree trunk had a rock placed in the fork to mark the treasure. Perry did not find the treasure and left for St. Louis to see his partner. Perry was shot and killed shortly thereafter. In 1878, a man named Medlin was working as a sheepherder in the area. He was said to have found the smelter, then the pin oak with the rock in the tree fork. He reportedly dug all over a high hill about one-half mile north of the key landmarks but never found any treasure. He finally gave up and left the country. The treasure could be in Llano County, Mason County or McCulloch County.

Jim Bowie's Lost Silver Mines

See Menard County.

Lead Balls Treasure

See Menard County.

Los Mina de las Almagres Mining District/Lost San Saba Mine/ Lost Almagres Mine/Lost Amarillas Mine

See Llano County.

Lost Iguanas Mine/Lost Mina de las Iguanas

See Menard County.

San Saba Junction Treasure

A San Saba treasure was supposed to be located near an old oak tree with an iron spike in it, north and east of the junction of the San Saba River and Colorado River. It could be Lampasas County or Mills County.

SCHLEICHER COUNTY

Bullion Cache

See Kimble County.

Little Llano Lost Mine and Treasure

See Llano County.

SCURRY COUNTY

Lost Conquistador Treasures/Spider Rock Treasures

See Stonewall County.

A treasure was said to have been hidden near Fort Griffin. *Library of Congress.*

SHACKLEFORD COUNTY

Collins Creek Treasure

A spring on Collins Creek near the Collins Place may mark a treasure cache. Its owner was killed, so his treasure was said to remain. It could be near Fort Griffin, which is on the Clear Fork of the Brazos River.

Hubbard Creek Treasure

Two Mexican bandits reportedly hid $50,000 worth of gold loot close to the Greer Place between Albany and Baird near Hubbard Creek. The bandits were captured and never able to recover their loot. It may be in Callahan County.

SHELBY COUNTY

Mexican Attoyac Bayou Cache

See Nacogdoches County.

STARR COUNTY

Carrie A. Thomas

Carrie A. Thomas, an American steamer, sank on June 16, 1880, off Rio Grande City with $125,000 or $140,000 in gold coins and bullion. Gold and silver coins have been recovered from the north bank of the Rio Grande, which may be from this wreck.

Casa de Bob Cache

Gold coins were said to have been cached near Rio Grande City.

Pancho Villa Treasures

Pancho Villa reportedly hid part of $1.5 million or $500,000 in the Roma area, according to Delores Agilero Vasquez, who was seventy-six when she gave a sworn deposition in the Imperial County Hospital at El Centro, California. No treasure was found. *See* Bexar County, "Pancho Villa Treasures"; Kleberg County, "Cinenia Caches/Pancho Villa Treasures"; and Nueces County, "Pancho Villa Treasures."

Rawhide Bag Treasure

Supposedly hidden under a mesquite tree near the Rio Grande below Roma was a rawhide bag full of Mexican gold and silver coins.

Roma Treasure

Near Roma, about half a million dollars was said to have been stashed in a lime pit.

STEPHENS COUNTY

Lost Mexican Caravan Treasure

About seven miles east of Breckinridge, a Mexican caravan treasure was rumored to be hidden on the Pugh Ranch.

Lost Platinum Mine

Indians were said to have discovered a platinum deposit north of Breckinridge. Several miners may have been killed at the mine site.

Sam Bass Breckenridge Treasure

Sam Bass supposedly buried $5,000 near Breckenridge before he was killed at Round Rock in 1878. It might now be located under Hubbard Creek Reservoir. Bass and his gang had a hideout on Big Caddo Creek, about fifteen miles from Breckinridge. Posses chased the gang out of the area after running gunfights.

STERLING COUNTY

Tower Hill Treasure

About eight miles from Sterling City at the old fort on Tower Hill, treasure hunters reportedly found some treasure and artifacts.

STONEWALL COUNTY

Aztec Treasure

Gold and silver Aztec treasure worth $10 million to $18 million supposedly was cached under an old Spanish mission's chapel, possibly a few miles north of Aspermont. The Aztec treasure included a large gold sun god image. Said to be near the Brazos River. This is one of many Aztec treasure legends that abound in the southwestern United States.

Lost Conquistador Treasures/Spider Rock Treasures

Part of the legendary Inca treasure that Spaniard Francisco Pizzaro's men looted from the Incas was reportedly cached in a hole seven varas deep near Double Mountain Fork of the Los Brazos de Dios (Double Mountain Fork of the Brazos River) near Double Mountain. According to legends, the cache included forty-nine mule loads of gold, silver, jewelry, jewels and gold Inca statues worth $60 million to $100 million, as well as an old Bible. The story was that some members of the Pizzaro Incan expedition deserted with this loot. In Texas, the survivors reportedly cached the treasure in twenty-one different holes when Indians attacked them. They also were afraid that other Spaniards from Pizarro's force would attack them. Survivors reportedly made a map and disappeared after hiding their treasure.

In northeastern Stonewall County, several skeletons, Spanish armor and artifacts were found in the early 1800s. People also found what they thought were treasure markers. After the Civil War, an old Spaniard with a rawhide map bought some land there. He dug a lot of holes and disappeared. A young Spaniard with a rawhide map came to the area and hired people to dig fifteen-foot-deep holes. They uncovered four skeletons at one location. The young Spaniard ran out of money and departed.

About 1903, Walter Leach found $12,000 in gold and Spanish artifacts in the area in some small caches. In 1909, Dave Arnold had a parchment map and dug extensively. A key marker was called spider rock, which was a rock with carved spokes and emblems.

About 1920, Frank D. Olmsted had a treasure map and bought land based on it. He dug many holes without finding anything. A six-pound gold ingot was rumored to have been recovered in this area. Southwest of Double Mountain, three Spanish chests containing church plate, jewelry, candlesticks and candles were also allegedly cached. This was reported as being one mile north of Rule. A Spanish mission reportedly had three old smelters and an abandoned gold mine in the area. Two silver statues, two silver crosses and silver arrowheads were found in the area. There is a similar story in Callahan County regarding a Spider Rock, with Dave Arnold also involved. Tom Penfield's *A Guide to Treasure in Texas* has several pages on this story. Steve Wilson's book *The Spider Rock Treasure* has a lot of information. *See* Callahan County, "Spider Rock Treasure." This could be in Kent County or Scurry County.

Lost Double Mountains Spanish Mine

A lost Spanish mine was supposedly located near the Double Mountains (thirteen miles southwest of Aspermont) close to the Salt and Double Mountain Fork. It could have been a copper mine, but some stories indicated it was a gold mine. It is probably the same gold mine discussed under "Lost Conquistador Treasures/Spider Rock Treasures."

The Brazos River and its tributaries have many tales of lost Spanish mines and treasure.
National Archives.

Lost Longest Lead Mine

See King County.

Salted Silver Mine

A salted silver mine was said to have caused a mining rush in Aspermont, which ended when the mine turned out to be nonproductive.

SUTTON COUNTY

Bullion Cache

See Kimble County.

Little Llano Lost Mine and Treasure

See Llano County.

TARRANT COUNTY

Benbrook Lake Cache

About 1925, a cache of $35,000 in gold coins was reportedly put in a milk can and buried near Benbrook, southwest of Fort Worth. An old man told police in the 1950s that he buried the cache about 1925 after taking it from a dead man. Benbrook Lake was later constructed and the site is thought to be underwater now.

William Riddle Cache

Farmer William Riddle reportedly hid $100,000 ($50,000), which was unaccounted for after he died in 1928. It was thought to be on or near his ranch near Fort Worth. Cash spent by his sons reportedly smelled musty. Riddle and his wife died without ever disclosing to their family where the money was hidden. One story was that robbers buried money in a lunch pail on his ranch, some five hundred yards from the ranch house. Riddle found the money, and the two outlaws attacked the ranch house to recover it. Riddle killed one, but two escaped. At least one of the escaped robbers later died. Could also be in Denton, Parker or Wise Counties.

TAYLOR COUNTY

Buffalo Gap Cache

About fifteen miles south of Abilene at Buffalo Gap gold coins, were supposedly cached by California Gold Rush 49ers returning from California. Indians attacked and killed them all.

Cedar Gap Loot

South of Abilene in the 1850s, an outlaw band may have hidden $107,000 from four bank robberies under a downed tree on the east side of West Mountain, which is part of Cedar Gap Mountain.

TERRELL COUNTY

Lost Hughes Gold Mine

This lost mine was supposed to be in the Dryden area.

Sanderson Loot

See Brewster County.

Spanish Gold Cave

Near where Independence Creek joins the Pecos River, there was a legend that Spaniards hid gold in a cave. Indians chased the Spaniards away. The Spaniards never returned for their gold. A Mexican reportedly found the cave and retrieved a gold bar but later returned it to the cave. Ranchers trying to get rid of rattlesnakes were said to have dynamited the cave entrance. It could be in Crockett County.

Train Robbery Loot

The diary of an outlaw indicated the loot from a 1912 train heist was cached near the Dryden stockyards. Others think it was located near Stockton, Pecos County, or Anderson, Grimes County. It could be in McCulloch County.

TOM GREEN COUNTY

Concho Cave Treasure

In 1887, in a cave close to the Concho River, a Fort Concho soldier was said to have found a skeleton and sacks of gold coins. This was rumored to be between the North Concho River and Middle Concho River. He covered the cave entrance with stones. He was then transferred from Fort Concho, supposedly to the Philippines, and was never able to later locate the cave. His

A Fort Concho soldier was said to have found treasure in a cave but was unable to relocate it. *Library of Congress.*

brother was given information about the cache but never found the treasure. In the early 1920s, this tale was found in a clock. U.S. troops did not occupy the Philippines until the Spanish-American War in 1898, making it unlikely that the soldier in the story was transferred there.

Outlaw San Angelo Treasure

Loot was rumored to be hidden in a cave on the south side of the Concho River not far from San Angelo.

Sheep Ranch Treasure

Near Christoval, $40,000 in gold coins was supposedly hidden.

TRAVIS COUNTY

Fort Colorado Caches

Near Fort Colorado (Fort Prairie), several treasures reportedly were cached.

Mexican Church Treasure

Near Mount Bonnel, a legend claimed a Mexican church treasure was hidden.

Montezuma Leander Treasure

See Williamson County.

Sam Bass Cave Cache

In a cave he used as a hideout near McNeil, southwest of Round Rock, outlaw Sam Bass was said to have cached $30,000 in gold.

Seven or Eight Mule Loads of Treasure

A legend indicated seven or eight mule loads of Mexican church treasure was cached near Austin by outlaws who were later killed by Indians. Another version of this story has seven or eight mule loads of bullion hidden in a Dagger Hollow cave due to Indians following the outlaws. One story was that a farmer, Hamlin, recovered the treasure and destroyed the flat stone with markings that indicated the location of this treasure cave as well as where seventy-five mule loads of bullion were said to have been hidden in a cave near the Colorado River. This other treasure story follows, under "Seventy-Five Mule Loads of Treasure."

Seventy-Five Mule Loads of Treasure

J. Frank Dobie was told this Spanish treasure legend by Wes Burton. When the Spanish were told to abandon their mines in the San Saba region, they hid the mines and moved their bullion. Unable to transport all the bullion, they supposedly hid seventy-five mule loads of gold and silver ore worth $6 million. May have been hidden northwest of Austin and southeast of Round Mountain close to the Colorado River.

Shoal Creek Treasures

Santa Anna's treasure of sixteen thousand doubloons ($200,000 to $260,000 in 1894 dollars; $3 million or more in modern value) was rumored to be on Shoal Creek near the Colorado River close to Austin. In 1836, during Santa Anna's invasion of rebellious Texas, several Mexican soldiers were said to have stolen a Mexican army payroll and then killed one another over the treasure. The lone survivor returned to Mexico, where he made a map with the treasure directions. According to the story, the treasure was cached five feet deep near a live oak tree with two eagle wings carved on it. Fiction writer O. Henry (William Sydney Porter), who lived in Austin, hunted for this treasure and wrote a short story about a search for this treasure. One Austin politician reportedly committed suicide after he embezzled money to buy a treasure map to this treasure.

Another treasure of $80,000 in gold coins was also said to have been hidden on Shoal Creek before Union forces arrived in Austin. This treasure was supposedly dug up in 1927, according to a newspaper account.

Spanish Miners' Treasure

See Williamson County.

Steinheimer's Millions

See Bell County.

TRINITY COUNTY

Apple Springs Cache

Near Apple Springs, a cache of gold coins was rumored to have been hidden near the Neches River. It could be in Angelina County.

Mexican or Spanish Cache

A legend indicated that near Trinity, a Mexican or Spanish treasure (gold coins or silver) from a pack train was cached. Indians attacked their camp between the Navasota River and Trinity River. The three survivors reached San Antonio. Many years later, one survivor returned to hunt unsuccessfully for the treasure. A few coins have been found in the area.

Mexican Stash

See Live Oak County.

TYLER COUNTY

Boone's Ferry Treasures

In 1836, after the Battle of San Jacinto, Mexican forces at Nacogdoches reportedly fled with nine burro loads of gold. Near Boone's Ferry (also called Belt's Ferry, after Samuel T. Belt's trading post) at the Neches River, they filled one of their cannon barrels with treasure and rolled it into the river from a bluff near Fort Teran before Texas rebels overtook them. One version said the cannon contained $60,000 worth of gold coins, while another version said $1 million. Fort Teran was situated three miles west of Rockland on the south side (north side, by some accounts) of the Neches River. Another story was that three pack loads of treasure were cached in a grove of trees on the nearby Neches River. A young Mexican came to the area in 1875 looking for the treasure, as his grandfather was one of the three Mexican soldiers involved in hiding the treasure. Two of the three soldiers who buried the treasure had died by then. The survivor gave a map to his grandson, who also said a chest of money was buried nearby between an oddly shaped rock and two pine trees (long gone by 1875) at Money Hill. These treasures could be in Angelina County or Jasper County.

Indian Gold Mine

Indians traded gold to settlers from their secret mine reportedly located on a bluff on the Neches River. It could be in Angelina County or Jasper County.

UPSHUR COUNTY

Colonel Bolton's Gold

On his plantation north of Gilmer, Colonel Ebenezer Bolton was said to have hidden barrels of gold coins before dying in 1877. After arriving in Texas in the 1850s, he developed a two-thousand-acre plantation and was known to have a large amount of gold coins.

Mexican Agents Treasure

Near Little Cypress Creek north of Gilmer, Mexican agents supposedly hid gold and silver coins after Texas became independent of Mexico. The Mexican agents tried to bribe Cherokees and other Indians to revolt against the new nation of Texas. The Cherokees were later driven from this area. This treasure could be in Morris County.

UPTON COUNTY

Castle Gap Treasures/Maximilian Treasure

According to a legend, where the Spanish Trail crossed the Pecos River, a wagonload of gold ore was being transported to Mexico. The gold ore was buried when Indians attacked. Other treasure from a later period was also supposedly hidden at or near Castle Gap about fifteen miles east of where the Spanish Trail crossed the Pecos River near the Upton-Crane County line.

Austrian Mexican emperor Maximilian's treasure was reportedly hidden near Castle Gap in 1866. Maximilian had been put on the Mexican throne

Mexican emperor Maximilian, who was Austrian, was said to have had his treasure stolen and buried in Texas. *Library of Congress.*

by primarily French emperor Napoleon III, as the Mexican government owed millions of dollars to Europeans. European royalty wanted to get repaid, so they tried to take over Mexico. Maximilian's armies were being defeated by the Juaristas in Mexico, so Maximilian's forces decided to move treasure from Mexico through Texas to the coast for transport to Europe. One tale said a party of four Austrian cavalry officers and possibly fifteen Mexicans with fifteen (or five) oxen team wagons carried gold, silver and jewelry (silver plate and ingots) from Mexico through El Paso. The treasure was in flour barrels, with a layer of flour on top. Six ex-Confederate soldiers, primarily from Missouri, joined the party to escort them through dangerous country. One version of the story has Tom Knight as the leader of the ex-Confederates, with Henry Stewart, Will Hart, Paul Naughton, Robert Lee Phillips and Wallace Jones being the other ex-Confederates. Other versions of this story have other names for the ex-Confederates, such as Will Carter, Earl Fisk, Bill Wooton and Bert Compton. The ex-Confederates discovered the treasure in the barrels and killed most of Maximilian's party (nineteen men). Maximilian's treasure was supposedly buried in a dry lake bed near Castle Gap, about fifteen miles east of the Horsehead Crossing of the Pecos River. All the wagons were burned over the burial place. The treasure was reportedly worth $4 to $5 million.

One of the ex-Confederates, Will Hart (Bert Compton), was shot by his companions and left to die, as he was ill, and his partners feared he would double-cross them if they left him behind. Hart made his way to Big Lake.

He returned with others to Castle Gap and discovered his five companions had been all murdered by Comanches. Later, Hart camped with some horse thieves, and they were all captured and jailed in San Angelo. Dr. Bradford Walters took care of Hart after attorney Henry Jamison got Hart released from jail. Hart was dying and drew a map and told the story of Maximilian's lost gold to Dr. Walters and Jamison. The two men took Hart's map when he died but were unable to find the treasure. They located a tall rock Hart had talked about. There are stories that iron remains of burned-out wagons, as well as harnesses and other material, have been found at Horsehead Crossing over the years.

Another version of this story is that in 1867, Clell Shephard and Oliver Shephard hid fifteen chests of gold in sandstone cliffs on the north side of the Pecos River near Horsehead Crossing. They returned each December to get enough gold to last them a year. In 1887, they both died in a farm accident in Jackson County, Missouri.

John S. Potter Jr.'s *The Treasure Diver's Guide* story (based on Dee Woods and Florence E. Shaner's book, *Blaze of Gold*) was a lot different. In this version of the story, there were fourteen Austrians and fifty pro-Maximilian soldiers protecting the treasure hidden in flour barrels. A group of ex-Confederates attacked the treasure wagon train. Two Austrians survived the attack and fled. Upon returning to Castle Gap with an armed force, the Austrians recovered the buried treasure and took it to Corpus Christi Bay. After the treasure was put on a boat, a storm sank the boat. *See* Nueces County, "Maximilian's Treasure."

Another lost treasure at Castle Gap was said to have been hidden about 1860, when the Butterfield Stage was robbed by outlaws of gold and silver allegedly bound for U.S. military posts and forts. The stagecoach was overturned into a ravine. One version has the driver, guard and passengers all killed and robbed. A cavalry patrol was supposedly spotted. The outlaws hid their plunder in a cave about one hundred yards from the robbery. The cave opening was hidden with rocks piled in front. All the outlaws were killed in a battle with the army except for one of the outlaw's slaves. The slave was held until the Civil War. In 1868, the former slave was said to have returned with a group of men to look for the lost loot, but everything had changed. The site of the overturned stage was found, and a few coins were recovered at the site. The cave and its treasure were not found.

There have been many searches for the treasures in and around Castle Gap. Emperor Maximilian is documented to have sent most of the royal jewelry and wealth home via his trusted aide Stefan Herzfeld, who put them aboard the Austrian corvette *Dondolo* at Veracruz. These ended up in the hands of Austrian emperor Franz Joseph, Maximilian's brother. Other valuables ended up in the protection of a few people or were given as payment for outstanding debts before Emperor Maximilian was captured and executed by the Juaristas on June 19, 1867. Much of the Castle Gap area has been dug up over the years. In 1969, one group used bulldozers to excavate to bedrock based on divining rod readings. Jeff W. Henderson's article in *Treasure World* revealed that in the Castle Gap area, he found seven coins dated 1781 to 1865, which he thought could have been part of Maximilian's treasure. One coin was from Guatemala and the rest were from Mexico. This could be in Crane County. See Pecos County, "Shephard Brothers Loot."

Cave Gold

Twenty chests of gold bullion were said to have been hidden in a cave about seventy miles southwest of Big Spring on a slight rise. A flat rock covered the cave entrance. The cave was reportedly found in the early 1900s but was lost again. This could be a Midland County location.

Rattlesnake Cave Treasure

Southeast of Castle Gap in a dry gulch, rich gold ore was supposed to have been hidden.

UVALDE COUNTY

Camp Wood Spanish Treasure and Lead-Silver Mines

See Real County.

Hoffman's Lead Mine

Hoffman's lead mine was said to have been north of Sabinal. In the 1850s, Hoffman was a rancher along the Sabinal River who had come to Texas from California. He used the lead from this deposit to make bullets. He was going to retire from ranching and mine lead but was killed by Indians.

Lost Ana Cacho Mountains Treasure

See Kinney County.

Lost Quicksilver Deposit/Lost Rangers Mine

A mercury (cinnabar) deposit was reportedly discovered and misplaced in the 1870s by a group of Texas Rangers who camped about four miles north of Sabinal on the Sabinal River. Thirty years later, several rangers returned to the area to look for the mercury. They made a deal with the owner of the land where they thought the mercury was located. After digging, they found nothing, so they abandoned the effort.

Silver Ledge of the Frio

Legends indicated a silver ledge may be located in Frio Canyon near Uvalde on the Frio River. Comanches supposedly found it and showed it to a Mexican boy they had captured. The Mexican boy escaped and was leading a party to the ledge when he died of illness. He made a rough map to the ledge and gave it to a man named Whitey. Whitey's brother-in-law was supposed to have located the silver ledge but died in a fight.

Tom Wall Treasure

See Real County.

Treasure Cave

Near Uvalde, a legend claimed a cave contained valuable ore and gold coins.

Turkey Creek Cache

A treasure cache was rumored to have been hidden on the road from Uvalde to Los Moros at the Turkey Creek crossing in an elm tree grove.

VAL VERDE COUNTY

Found Bullion

Close to the Old Spanish Trail on the east bank of Mud Creek, two or four Spanish bullion bars were recovered. The Old Spanish Trail ran from Mexico to San Antonio. At the mouth of the Pecos River, it crossed the Rio Grande, traveled to the Devil's River, passed Seminole Hill, and east of Del Rio, crossed Mud Creek.

Mexican Loma Alta Cache

Near Loma Alta, a legendary Mexican cache of gold bars was stashed. It could be in Edwards County.

Montez Rodriguez Cache

A $75,000 ($37,500 to $74,000) cache of silver coins and jewels (opals) was reportedly hidden near Shumia by a Cuban lady, Montez Veronica Rodriguez, and two men, Pronto Green and Dirk Pacer, who fled from Mexico with their ill-gotten gains in 1881. Montez Rodriguez became sick and suddenly died after crossing into Texas. She was buried in a grave with a stone with her initials, M.R., carved on it, in a side canyon not far from the Pecos River. Near the grave, the two men supposedly buried silver ingots and jewelry to reduce their burden. After crossing into Indian Territory (now Oklahoma), Dirk Pacer died after becoming ill in the Kiamichi Mountains. In Kansas, Pronto Green was killed in a train wreck. Before he died, Green told the whole story of the lost treasure to those caring for him.

Montezuma Sugar Loaf Mountain Treasure

In a cave near Sugar Loaf Mound or Sugar Loaf Mountain near Del Rio, another legend indicated Montezuma's Aztec treasure was cached.

Painted Cave Treasure

Near Painted Cave, a treasure was supposedly cached near Del Rio.

Pecos Canyon Treasure

This treasure was rumored to be near Dorso.

Presidio de Altar Treasure

A legend indicated this treasure was cached around six miles north of old Fort Hudson, as well as nineteen miles south of Juno and twenty-one miles north of Comstock.

Seminole Hill Treasure Cave

While herding sheep near Seminole Hill, Mexican sheepherder Santiago reportedly found a small cave full of Spanish gold bullion and coins. The sight scared him so much that he never returned to recover the treasure.

Snively's Lost Mine

In 1866, Major Jacob Snively reported that he found a rich mine near the Rio Grande in the Sierra Nevada Mountains. He raised an expedition, which was attacked by Indians. In 1867, Snively commanded a larger expedition of about one hundred men. No gold was found, and the expedition split up. They traveled down to where the Pecos River emptied into the Rio Grande and searched near Eagle Springs. This mine could be in Coryell County.

Spanish Fort Devil's River Treasure

Spanish treasure from Spanish Fort supposedly was hidden on the east bank of the Devil's River.

Spanish Well Treasure

Old Spanish coins were reportedly hidden in a well with stone sides on a bluff between the Rio Grande and Del Rio, some 150 yards from the Devil's River. A grave was close by.

Victoria County

Lafitte Lavaca Bay Treasure

See Calhoun County.

Lafitte Lavaca Treasures

See Jackson County.

Mexican Families Treasure

See Calhoun County.

Moro's Money

About 1859 or 1860, a man called Moro, possibly a Spaniard, came to the Rose family's Buena Vista Plantation on the Guadalupe River about seven miles south of Victoria. He stayed for several months and left. He gave gifts of gold coins to the slaves. He reportedly dug at night near the plantation. Many thought he found the treasure he was looking for. Another version was that his gold was cached there near a large fig tree. Later, he reportedly went to Mexico, where he was hanged as a spy.

Waller County

Buried Mexican Payroll

In 1836, Mexican soldiers reportedly transported silver on five mules bound for General Santa Anna's army. When the soldiers learned that Santa Anna had been defeated at San Jacinto and that Texas troops were nearby, they buried the silver just north of Katy before fleeing to Mexico. They used a big black granite rock to mark the burial place and made a map. They later traded the map for supplies and horses from a rancher. The rancher died, and the map was later lost. This treasure could be in Harris County.

Ward County

Chief Yellow Wolf Treasure

Comanche chief Yellow Wolf was said to have hidden silver ore and coins in the Monahans area. Supposedly, when he was buried, three mule loads of gold and silver were buried with him. It could be in Crane County, Ector County or Winkler County.

Montezuma Pecos Treasure

See **Reeves County**.

Pecos River La Mina Perdida (The Lost Mine)/Lost Perdida Mine

See **Reeves County**.

Wagon Train Cache

A treasure from a gold-laden California Gold Rush 49ers wagon train massacre was supposedly buried north of Monahans. Another possible location is about fifteen miles west of Pyote on a hill overlooking the Pecos River. An old fort may be located in the area. During the early 1900s, a Mexican found a wooden box with treasure in a cone-shaped hill. Other treasure was thought to be nearby. It could be in Winkler County. This may be same story as Winkler County, "Gold Nuggets Cache."

Washington County

Southern Pacific Loot

A legend claimed outlaws robbed a Southern Pacific train in 1891 and hid the loot not far from Samuels in the Bullis Crossing area. The outlaws were killed before they could recover their loot. See Brewster County, "Sanderson Loot," as likely the same story on different sides of the state.

WEBB COUNTY

Dario Gonzales Loot

Dario Gonzales was said to have buried $500,000 worth of loot near the Loyas Ranch Settlement not far from Laredo. It could be on either side of the Rio Grande.

Shipp Ranch Treasure

Near Aguilares (Eagle's Nest) on the Shipp Ranch, a cowboy's horse stepped into a hole. The cowboy reportedly discovered that the horse's hoof had smashed into a container (box or trunk) filled with Spanish doubloons just below the surface. The cowboy took what his horse could carry, but some coins were left behind. He returned to the Shipp Ranch and started a stampede of ranch hands looking for the rest of the stash. The cowboy and his friends couldn't locate the rest of the coins.

WHARTON COUNTY

General Vincente Filisola Treasure

A legend indicated that after Santa Anna's defeat at San Jacinto, Mexican general Vincente Filisola buried treasure at Spanish Camp before he and his men retreated to Mexico.

Lost Spanish Treasure Cannon

See Lavaca County.

WHEELER COUNTY

Mobeetee Stagecoach Loot

Several chests of silver coins taken in an 1867 robbery were said to have been buried within a half mile of Mobeetee.

Near Fort Elliott, a paymaster reportedly hid his funds. *Library of Congress.*

Paymaster Cache

A paymaster's treasure was reportedly near Fort Elliott not far from Mobeetee near a draw under a willow tree.

WILLACY COUNTY

Espiritu Santo

The Spanish ship *Espiritu Santo* was part of the 1554 fleet that sank in a hurricane. A diver found the wreck about 1964. Platoro Limited Inc. of Indiana and Quest Geo-Marine out of California explored this ship and others off Padre Island. Platoro operated for three months, salvaging a small gold cross, a gold bar, several silver discs, several crossbows, cannons and three astrolabes. Hurricane Beulah stopped Platoro's recovery efforts. The Texas attorney general filed a lawsuit claiming all the salvage for the State of Texas. The Texas Land Commissioners Office was given control over about $3 million worth of treasure and artifacts. This site is in the Mansfield Cut Underwater Archeological District. See chapter 2, "Spanish Treasure Ships."

San Estevan *Salvage*

The two-hundred-ton Spanish nao *San Estevan* under Captain Francisco del Mecerno was part of the 1554 fleet that sank in a hurricane. Several months after sinking, it was partially salvaged by the Spanish. The Texas Antiquities

Committee did salvage on the wreck in 1972–73 and later. There was 1.5 meters of sand and shells over much of the site. Over twelve thousand kilograms of encrusted artifacts were recovered. Now the wreck is in the Mansfield Cut Underwater Archeological District. Part of the treasure is on exhibit in the Corpus Christi Museum of Science and History. See chapter 2, "Spanish Treasure Ships."

Santa Maria de Yciar

Spanish salvage techniques such as this were used to recover treasure off Padre Island. *National Park Service.*

The Spanish two-hundred-ton ship *Santa Maria de Yciar* was part of the 1554 fleet that sank in a hurricane. In 1957, dredging operations for the Mansfield Channel, which cuts through Padre Island, destroyed much of this shipwreck. Coins, timbers and other parts and cargo of the ship ended up in the dredge spoils and even clogged the dredge pipe. An anchor was recovered. This site is in the Mansfield Cut Underwater Archeological District.

Texas Navy Silver Bars

See Cameron County.

WILLIAMSON COUNTY

Chief Yellow Wolf's Lost Mine

See Llano County.

Mexican Round Rock Mine

In the Round Rock area, a lost Mexican silver mine may be located.

Montezuma Leander Treasure

In a cave near Leander, a Montezuma treasure of $30 million in gold bars was supposedly cached. It could be in Travis County.

Padre San Gabriel Treasure

Spanish padres were rumored to have hidden a mission treasure on the San Gabriel River. The treasure markers were swept away by a flood.

Round Rock Silver Ore Cache

Near Round Rock silver ore was reportedly cached.

Sam Bass Round Rock Loot

In or near a cave south of Round Rock, outlaw Sam Bass reportedly hid loot. A map, on the other hand, indicated Bass put loot in a hollow tree on the Leander–Liberty Bell Road some two miles northwest of Round Rock. Using the map, a treasure hunter chopped down a tree at that location, but it only had a rusty nail in it.

Spanish Miners' Treasure

Forty mule loads of silver bars from a Spanish silver mine near Fort Croghan, Burnet County, were rumored to have been cached near Leander by Spanish miners when Comanche Indians attacked them. A legend had the treasure hidden on the Davis (Dorrah) Farm in a seventeen-by-seventeen-by-one-hundred-foot hole. Although a Spanish axe was found in the shaft, there was no treasure. The shaft was filled in around 1925 or 1935. *See* Burnet County, "Lost Spanish Silver Mine."

WINKLER COUNTY

Chief Yellow Wolf Treasure

See Ward County.

Gold Nuggets Cache

A gold nuggets cache was said to have been hidden in a mine shaft about fifteen miles southeast of Kermit. One version of this tale had miners being trailed by Indians. The miners hid the gold and were later unable to find it.

Wagon Train Cache

See Ward County.

WISE COUNTY

Bridgeport Lost Mine

A lead and silver mine was rumored to be south of Bridgeport near a creek.

Bridgeport Stagecoach Loot

A stagecoach robbery occurred near Bridgeport, with the gold said to have been buried north of a stagecoach stop outside of Bridgeport.

Devil's Den Treasures

In the area of Devil's Den near Bridgeport, $200,000 in gold coins was supposedly cached during an Indian attack. Also, a hermit was said to have hidden money in a cave in the Devil's Den area.

Routh's Cache

About 1870 or 1871, rancher H.C. Routh told his daughter Mary Elizabeth he was going to bury his life savings on a creek bank between a couple of trees, over the rise from his house. Routh lived outside of Decatur. Later, when he left his home to pay his taxes, Routh was ambushed and killed, and the tax money was stolen. His life savings was said to have never been found.

Sam Bass Wise Creek Treasure

A Sam Bass treasure was said to be near Wise Creek. It could also be in Parker County.

William Riddle Cache

See Tarrant County.

Young County

Andy Duke Treasure

Near Fort Belknap, a priest called Andy K. Duke supposedly hid a Spanish mission's gold and silver in a vault he constructed. An old map reportedly indicated the cache was near a spring with a rock shaped like a finger pointing to it.

Fort Belknap Bank Loot

Five outlaws reportedly robbed a Monterrey, Mexico, bank in 1886. Mexican lawmen killed two outlaws before they reached the Rio Grande and were hot on the trail of the others. Texas Rangers then encountered the outlaws and killed two more. One outlaw evaded the law and made his way to the Clear Fork of the Red River. Being near Fort Belknap, he decided to hide $18,000 in gold coins about one mile north of or near the fort. The outlaw later was shot and two cowboys, Bellas Carter and Jackson, encountered him on the ground twenty miles south of Roswell, New Mexico, at a Pecos River crossing. Jackson went to get a doctor. The dying outlaw reportedly left information about the treasure in a note or waybill and verbally informed Carter about the hidden loot. The robbers had left a wagon rod in the ground to help mark the site. Carter later wrote that he hid the loot 256 or 252 steps north of a creek and 86 steps west of a cactus along a shallow fork.

Outlaws reportedly hid $18,000 near Fort Belknap. *Library of Congress.*

A ring of three rocks marked the location. Carter reportedly found the site but was chased off by the landowner. Carter hid the ring of rocks from the landowner before he left. When Carter snuck back, he was unable to locate the ring or the treasure.

ZAPATA COUNTY

Stone Fort Treasure

On the Rio Grande, about a mile north of San Ygnacio, was a settlement and fort destroyed by floods. A treasure was said to have been hidden nearby.

ZAVALA COUNTY

Cassidy's Gold

See Maverick County.

Espantosa Lake Treasures

See Dimmit County.

Loma de Sauce Treasure

A treasure of $25,000 in gold coins was supposedly hidden about three miles north of or near the Nueces River. The treasure was said to have been buried with two murdered priests.

Turkey Creek Treasure

Near Turkey Creek and La Pryor, a treasure was reportedly cached. Stonemason John Wyman thought a treasure was buried before the Civil War in an elm grove where a road crossed Turkey Creek.

Chapter 2

SPANISH TREASURE SHIPS

Spain developed a system of shipping goods and people from Spain to the Americas, with the fleet returning to Spain full of treasure, exotic cargo and successful, rich Spaniards. The Spanish Crown was always deeply in debt due to wars and its colonial enterprises. Returning treasure fleets were of vital importance to Spain.

The Flota in Veracruz, Mexico, took on stacks of gold and silver bars and coins from the mines of Guanajuato and Zacatecas. Two or more galleons could come from Manila every year across the Pacific to California and down the coast to Acapulco. From Acapulco, mahogany, silks, spices, diamonds, china and other exotic goods would be transported overland to Veracruz. From Central America to Veracruz came dyewoods, vanilla, opals, hides, pearls, etc. After loading the cargo, the fleet would lumber off on an eighteen-to-twenty-day voyage to Havana, Cuba.

Losses to the Spanish treasure fleets in their first twelve years of operation totaled more than 45 percent of the ships. The biggest danger to these awkward, cumbersome ships were hurricanes and storms. Many of these ships, carrying tons of gold, silver and goods, were lost. Pirates had bases in the Caribbean Sea, at Galveston Island, Texas, and in southern Louisiana during the Spanish wars of independence, which also claimed Spanish treasure ships.

One of the biggest disasters involved the 1554 Spanish fleet of four ships from the original 1553 fleet that had sailed from Spain. On April 29, 1554, a hurricane hit the New Spain Flota five days after it left Veracruz, Mexico, bound for Spain. The four ships were carrying about ninety-six thousand pounds of gold and silver. The *San Estevan (Esteban)* under Captain Francisco del Mecerno, the *Santa Maria de Yciar* under Captain Alonso Ozosi and the nao *Espiritu Santo* were shipwrecked off Padre Island at the present Mansfield Cut. Only the *San Andres* made it to Havana. It was too damaged to repair.

About one-half to two-thirds of the passengers and crew on the three shipwrecked vessels made it to shore. One small group of survivors took a small boat to go for help and managed to reach a Spanish settlement near Tampico. Most of the three hundred survivors tried to reach Spanish settlements to the south on foot, but all were massacred by Indians except for one priest who had been injured by arrows.

The Spanish rescue and salvage fleet of six vessels arrived within two months of the disastrous ship sinkings. Only the *San Estevan* was partially above water. One salvage ship sank in a storm, but 35,805 pounds of silver and gold were recovered, so most of the silver and gold was underwater and left behind. On Padre Island, over the years, many Spanish gold and silver coins and ingots from this disaster have been recovered. Parts of Padre Island are now in the Padre Island National Seashore Park.

The wreck of the *Espiritu Santo* was found about 1964, with gold, silver and artifacts salvaged over several years by Billy Kenon and the Znika brothers. The State of Texas claimed the vessel and its cargo and filed lawsuits against Platoro Limited Inc. The litigation ended in 1984 with the treasure finders getting only $313,000 from Texas and Texas keeping everything salvaged by the treasure hunters. The three wreck sites of the ships from the original 1554 fleet that was returning to Spain are now in the Mansfield Cut Underwater Archeological District. The *San Estevan* was partially excavated over several years. Part of the excavated treasure from recent times is on exhibit in the Corpus Christi Museum of Science and History and other museums. It is likely that treasure from this fleet still lies scattered along Padre Island. The ships probably broke apart, as has been found with many other wrecks of wooden treasure ships.

During the voyages from Veracruz to Havana, a number of Spanish treasure ships disappeared or were lost. Some likely were sunk off Padre Island and the Texas coast. Several rich Spanish treasure ships were reportedly captured and destroyed by Lafitte's pirates along the Texas coast.

Chapter 3

LOST MINES

*V*ery little gold has been mined in Texas. Gold has been found in the Llano District and West Texas, usually in small amounts associated with silver and copper mining. Traces of gold occur in the Shafter, Van Horn, Allamoore and Quitman Mountains areas. Gold has been mined in Howard, Irion, Llano, Taylor, Uvalde and Williamson Counties. Most stories of lost gold mines in other counties are questionable.

Silver, on the other hand, has been mined in a number of places in Texas. There could be much truth in stories regarding lost Texas silver mines. In the Llano Uplift geologic area in Llano, Mason and San Saba Counties, Spanish prospects and mines have been located. Some silver mining also took place on Silver Mine Creek, Gillespie County. The Presidio Mine near Shafter, Presidio County, produced more than thirty-two million ounces of silver, a small amount of gold and other minerals and was 4,000 feet in length and up to 1,500 feet deep. Silver mining occurred in the Spanish and Mexican period near El Paso. The Trans-Pecos mining area includes Brewster, Culberson, Hudspeth and Presidio Counties, with a number of small mines.

Lead (galena) and zinc (sphalerite) has been mined in Blanco, Brewster, Burnet, Culberson, Gillespie, Hudspeth and Presidio Counties. Lead and zinc were often byproducts associated with other minerals. East Texas, which has several lost lead mine stories, does not seem to have had any commercial lead mines, just scattered low-grade deposits.

The Spanish thirst for gold and silver resulted in many expeditions to explore new lands and conquer Indians. Spanish explorers from New Spain (now

Mexico) ventured into frontier areas looking for great wealth similar to what was found in the Central American Aztec empire and the South American Inca empire. All minerals on Spanish lands belonged to the Spanish Crown, but it was common for illegal gold and silver mining to occur to avoid paying the Spanish royalty. Much contraband treasure was transported to Spain over the years, as indicated by Spanish bullion recovered in modern times from those sunken Spanish shipwrecks that did not have the marks on ingots to show that the required royalty had been paid to the Spanish Crown. Often, there would be almost as much unregistered treasure on a ship as treasure registered with the Spanish Crown, for which the royalty had been paid.

Although slavery was illegal, many Indians were treated as slaves by the Spanish. Slave raiding expeditions by tribes friendly to the Spanish, as well as by Spanish settlers, were common in Spanish colonial times. In 1592, Spain made it illegal for priests to own and run mines and strengthened that law in 1621 due to the Jesuits trying to circumvent the law. In 1600, much silver was found by Spanish explorers and prospectors in Chihuahua and later in Senora. Many fortunes were made from these and other mines, which spurred further exploration and settlement along the northern New Spain frontier. Silver was transported through Texas on the Chihuahua Trail to Texas ports on the Gulf of Mexico.

Central Texas's San Saba River-Llano River area was said to have been used by the Apaches and Comanches as a source for almost pure silver for the jewelry and ornaments they wore and traded. Early Spanish explorers traveled through the region looking for gold and silver and named the San Saba River after Saint Sabbas, a sixth-century monk. In 1756, Lieutenant-General Don Bernardo de Miranda y Flores commanded a twenty-three-man expedition northwest from San Antonio to explore the country. Near Honey Creek, close to where the Llano River and Colorado River junction, they recovered three pounds of silver ore, which assayed ten ounces of silver per one hundred pounds of ore. They expected rich mines to be found in that region.

In 1757, Spanish soldiers, priests, miners and others from San Antonio established Mission San Saba (Mission Santa Cruz de San Saba) about three miles east of the of present Menard and founded San Saba Presidio (Presidio de San Luis de las Amarillas) a few miles west of present Menard. Legends indicated the mission priests found an Indian silver mine nearby and forced the Indians to mine the ore. This mine was known as the Los Almagres Mine. Legends tell of many lost mines in this area. *See* Llano County, "Los Mina de las Almagres Mining District/Lost San Saba Mine/

Lost Almagres Mine/Lost Amarillas Mine"; Menard County, "Lost Blanco Mine"; Menard County, "Lost Iguanas Mine/Lost Mina de las Iguanas"; and Menard County, "Jim Bowie's Lost Silver Mines."

For decades, Texas had few Spanish settlers due to Indian hostility, especially from the Comanches. Settlers and adventurers searched for lost and abandoned Spanish mines in the mountains and valleys. French traders and explorers also crossed the Red River from Louisiana into Texas after hearing of Indian mines along the Trinity River. Indian mines were often areas where rocks for weapons and implements, as well as pigments for paint, were mined by Indians.

Thousands of miners heading for California also began prospecting and mining along the way west. Americans discovered rich mines in many of the areas rumored to have contained lost Spanish mines or Indian mines in Arizona and New Mexico. The Indians resisted the American invasion of their lands, much as they had resisted the Spanish and Mexican invasions. Indian attacks caused many mines and settlements to be abandoned. At least fifty-four Texas counties have abandoned Spanish mine, lost mine and lost ledge stories.

Chapter 4

BORDER WARS

*I*n 1659, El Paso del Norte, Mexico, was established just across the Rio Grande from present-day El Paso, Texas. From here, Spain conquered New Mexico, but the Pueblo Revolt in 1680 caused the Spaniards to flee to El Paso del Norte after losing more than four hundred killed. In 1691, Diego de Vargas led a force of Spanish soldiers and Indian allies that recaptured New Mexico.

Spain established more permanent missions and forts in Texas to keep the French from claiming the land. French traders and explorers often crossed into Spanish-claimed Texas to trade and look for minerals. In 1690, Spaniard Alonso de Leon entered east Texas with Catholic missionaries, but the missions were unsuccessful. In 1718, San Antonio was settled by Spanish farmers and ranchers with a church called the Alamo and a presidio. San Antonio became the major Spanish settlement in Texas. From San Antonio, Spanish expeditions hunting for gold and silver were sent out. In Central Texas, San Saba Presidio and Mission San Saba were established on the San Saba River to move Spanish settlements northward and to engage in mining.

On March 16, 1758, about two thousand Comanche, Tonkawa and Hasinai (Caddo) Indians attacked and burned down Mission San Saba, killing two padres and several pro-Spanish Indians. The Indians besieged nearby San Saba Presidio. A Spanish relief force arrived, and the Indians retreated north.

A retaliation force from New Spain was put together to avenge the attack at San Saba. Colonel Diego Ortiz Parrilla led a force of about 139 Spanish

Mission San Saba was attacked and destroyed in 1758 and has lost silver mines nearby. *Wikipedia.*

soldiers, 241 militiamen, 254 pro-Spanish Indians, a couple of priests and two cannons north from San Antonio. They destroyed an Indian village on a fork of the Brazos River. Near present-day Spanish Fort, Parilla's army found large Wichita and Comanche camps, including a stockaded Wichita camp on the south side of the Red River with a French flag flying on a flagpole. About six thousand Indians attacked the Spanish force on October 7, 1759, in a four-hour battle. The Spanish lost their two cannons and nineteen killed in the Battle of the Two Villages. The Spanish army fled south to San Saba Presidio.

In 1761, stone walls replaced the timber walls at San Saba Presidio. From 1761 through 1768, about three hundred Spaniards and pro-Spanish Indians lived at the presidio. In 1768, the Spanish abandoned San Saba Presidio due to Indian attacks and unsuccessful agricultural and mining development.

Indian raids and wars in Texas continued into the 1880s, with many trading parties, settlements and travelers attacked. Many lost treasure and lost mine stories relate to Indian attacks from this period. Indians from Mexico as well as the Great Plains raided Texas for supplies and horses. The Texas-Mexico border was also plagued by outlaws and bandits.

Juan Cortina (Juan Nepomuceno Cortina Goseacochea) was called the Mexican Robin Hood and a great many other names. Cortina's family owned much land on both sides of the Rio Grande when the Mexican-American War caused difficulties for his family. He was a powerful Mexican governor, politician, rancher and brigadier general. Juan Cortina was rumored to have buried much treasure near his family's ranch at Santa Rita, near Brownsville. He engaged in personal wars against south Texas, called the First and Second Cortina Wars, in 1859 and 1861. He had other conflicts over the years with south Texas before he died in 1894. To many Texans, Juan Cortina was just another border bandit. *See* Cameron County, "Juan Nepomuceno Cortina Treasure."

Francisco "Pancho" Villa (born as Jose Doroteo Arango Arambula) was a bandit general who played a big part in the Mexican Revolution as a leader. His raid into Columbus, New Mexico, on March 9, 1916, caused the United States to invade Mexico to try to capture him. Villa was murdered on July 20, 1923, on the orders of President Alvaro Obregon, who was Villa's rival. On her deathbed in 1956, Delores Agilero Vasquez claimed Pancho Villa buried five treasures worth $1.5 million in Texas and more than $8 million in Mexico. Vasquez claimed to have once been a colonel in Pancho Villa's army. *See* Bexar County, "Pancho Villa Treasures"; El Paso County, "Pancho Villa Treasures"; Kleberg County, "Pancho Villa Cinenia Caches/Pancho Villa Treasure"; Nueces County, "Pancho Villa Treasures"; and Starr County, "Pancho Villa Treasure."

Chapter 5

TEXAS INDEPENDENCE AND THE MEXICAN-AMERICAN WAR TREASURE

*A*fter Mexican independence from Spain, Federalists and Centralists warred over the form of the new Mexican Republic and who would control it. In the Texas Revolution (War of Texas Independence), recent American colonists and tejanos (Mexicans native to Texas) revolted against a Mexican government under President General Antonio Lopez de Santa Anna. Santa Anna personally led the Mexican army to put down the Texas rebellion. He proclaimed all the rebels were pirates and that his army would take no prisoners.

General Jose de Urrea led a Mexican force along the Texas coast and took no prisoners. Santa Anna led another army to San Antonio, where he besieged and conquered the Alamo, killing all the Texas defenders. The Texas rebels were mostly newly arrived settlers and adventurers from the United States. Davy Crockett (an American politician and frontiersman) and Jim Bowie (of Lost Bowie Mine fame) were among those killed at the Alamo.

The Mexican army continued their advance as the disorganized Texans retreated northward in what was called the Runaway Scrape. Many families buried their money and valuables as they became refugees. General Urrea's Mexican army defeated several groups of Texans in a series of battles and usually executed any captured Texans. A Texan force at Goliad in Presidio La Bahia surrendered, with more than four hundred Texas rebels and their commander, Colonel James Fannin, executed on March 27, 1836.

Santa Anna continued his pursuit and camped on Buffalo Bayou just east of Houston. In the late afternoon of April 21, 1836, Sam Houston's

Texas army of about 900 attacked Santa Anna's unprepared camp. Santa Anna's army of about 1,200 soldiers was trapped and destroyed. About 650 Mexican soldiers were killed and 300 were captured, while Houston's Texas army only had 11 killed and about 30 wounded, including Sam Houston. *See* Harris County, "Santa Anna's San Jacinto Treasure."

In order to save his life, the captured Santa Anna surrendered on the Texans' terms. As part of his agreement, Santa Anna ordered the evacuation of all Mexican troops from Texas to points south of the Rio Grande under the Treaties of Velasco. Many stories of lost Mexican payrolls and refugee treasure came from this period in 1836. Counties with these lost treasure stories are Angelina, Caldwell, Calhoun, Colorado, Dimmit, Harris, Jasper, La Salle, Lavaca, McMullen, Nueces, Presidio, Randall, San Augustine, Refugio, Travis, Tyler, Waller and Wharton.

No large Mexican invasion of the new Republic of Texas occurred, as there were other revolts in Mexico to put down. The Republic of Mexico claimed Texas was its rebel province and not a free country. Raids were made by both sides on the border between Texas and Mexico, as the area between the Rio Grande and Nueces River (the Nueces Strip) was disputed territory. Lands to the west were also disputed.

On March 1, 1845, the United States annexed the Republic of Texas, which caused the United States and Mexico to go to war in 1846. General Arista and about 3,400 Mexican soldiers lost the Battle of Palo Alto on May 8, 1846. At the Battle of Resaca de la Palma the next day, the Mexican army was again defeated when American cavalry captured the Mexican artillery and baggage train. Both battles have legends of buried Mexican treasure. *See* Cameron County, "Battle of Resaca de la Palma Treasure" and Cameron County, "Mexican Army Payroll."

A series of disastrous defeats followed for Mexico, ending with the capture and occupation of Mexico City in 1847. The Treaty of Guadalupe-Hidalgo in 1848 ended the Mexican-American War. The United States-Mexico boundary became the Rio Grande.

Chapter 6

JESSE JAMES, OTHER OUTLAWS
AND THEIR LOOT

*I*nformation on Texas outlaws is hard to verify, as outlaws used many
aliases, moved around a lot and seldom told the truth. Outlaws were not
good people. They paid cash to poor farmers and ranchers to hide them
from authorities and to keep quiet. Much information has been accumulated
on famous outlaws since the 1950s, when interest in the Old West surged in
movies, books and magazines. There is a lot of conflicting information.

Before the widespread use of currency, outlaw loot consisted of gold and
silver coins and bullion too heavy to carry on a horse when a posse was chasing
the outlaws. After a robbery, the outlaws often split and individually buried
their share of the loot. If hard-pressed by a posse or lawmen, the outlaws
often buried or hid their loot not far from the robbery site and individually
rode in different directions to confuse their pursuers. Since outlaws usually
rode better horses than the posse or lawmen, they had an edge when escaping
if they weren't carrying too much weight. Sometimes outlaws had fresh horses
staked along their escape route. Many outlaws hid a number of small caches
of loot in different areas to retrieve later. Most outlaw loot stories are just about
the gang's leader. Gang members also hid their loot and often died with their
boots on, likely leaving behind hidden caches.

Jesse James and his brother Frank led the James Gang, which ranged over
large regions of the United States. The James Gang contained many ex-
Confederate soldiers who had ridden with rebel guerrilla leader William
Quantrill and other Confederate guerrillas. Frank Triplett's book *The Life,
Times and Treacherous Death of Jesse James* listed $263,278 in James Gang loot
from 1866 to 1881 from twenty train, bank and stagecoach robberies. It is

likely that individual members of the James Gang stole much more money also. Many robberies in that period were blamed on Jesse James, but he was often in another part of the country at that time. Jesse and Frank James had a married sister in north Texas, whom they were said to have visited a number of times. They also had several Texas hideouts.

Jesse James was murdered by Robert Ford in St. Joseph, Missouri, on April 3, 1882, for a $10,000 reward, but Ford only received a small part of it. Due to a combination of politics, Reconstruction animosities and legal tricks, Frank James was able to avoid prison, although he was jailed several times. Jesse James treasure stories include Culberson, Dallas, Grayson, Live Oak, Maverick and Pecos Counties. More James Gang treasure stories take place in Oklahoma, where some of their loot has actually been recovered.

Sam Bass was another successful outlaw whose gang robbed extensively in the Midwest. He was another cowboy who went outlaw. Sam Bass and his gang had a number of Texas hideouts. He committed robberies outside of Texas, as well as in north and central Texas. Sam Bass's most noted robbery was a train at Big Springs, Nebraska, on September 18, 1877, when his gang stole three boxes, each holding $20,000 in newly minted $20 gold pieces. Returning to north Texas near Fort Worth, Bass made the mistake of spending some of those freshly minted gold coins to get supplies. The store clerk notified the law. After a series of running gunfights with posses, the Bass Gang fled the area. It is likely Sam Bass and his gang cached the newly minted money. Needing money that was not newly minted, Sam Bass and his gang tried to rob a bank in Round Rock, just north of Austin. However, Jim Murphy, a Bass Gang member, told Texas Rangers about the heist in advance so he could get out of being prosecuted. Local lawmen and Texas Rangers intercepted the Bass Gang. Deputy Sheriff Maurice Moore and one of the outlaws were killed in the shootout, and another lawman was wounded. Sam Bass was fatally shot and died the next day on his twenty-seventh birthday, July 21, 1878. Legends claimed Sam Bass's loot was buried in Brewster, Cooke, Dallas, Denton, Llano, Mason, Montague, Parker, Stephens, Travis, Williamson and Wise Counties. It is likely that Sam Bass and his various gang members cached some of their loot, especially the newly minted $20 gold pieces, since the new coins marked them as being train robbers.

There were a number of outlaws and banditos in Texas robbing and pillaging Texas trails and roads. Texas Rangers and the U.S. Army played a big part in ending large-scale robberies. The Newton Gang spent some time in Texas and reportedly hid some treasure. *See* Bexar County, "Roundout Train Robbery Loot."

Chapter 7

JEAN LAFITTE AND PIRATES

Most lost Texas pirate treasure stories include Jean Lafitte, the famous pirate, privateer, slave trader and smuggler. He commanded a fleet of pirates or privateers who ranged far and wide in the Gulf of Mexico into the Caribbean Sea as well as Central America. His headquarters included Barataria Bay in Louisiana and Galveston Island, Texas. Often, he and his men sailed as privateers, under letters of marque from some Central American or South American country rebelling against Spain.

Jean Lafitte was chased out of his Louisiana base, where Lafitte and his pirates had helped defeat the British invasion at the Battle of New Orleans during the War of 1812. Jean Lafitte moved his base to Campeachy, on the east end of Galveston Island. The French pirate/privateer Louis-Michel Aury, was based on the west end of Galveston Island at Galvez Town. Aury attacked Spanish merchant ships during the various revolutions against Spain and served as the Mexican governor of the Galveston Island area. Aury left Texas to fight in the wars of Central America and South America before dying in 1821.

On Galveston Island, Lafitte had a fort, home and warehouse called Maison Rouge in Campeachy on Galveston Bay. Pirates anchored safely in Galveston Bay and ventured into the Gulf of Mexico to raid Spanish vessels and vessels from other countries. Campeachy was a base for revolutionaries, pirates and adventurers, as Mexico was in revolt against Spain, along with other Central American and South American areas that

Pirate Jean Lafitte had a Galveston Island headquarters. Many legends about his lost treasures cover the Texas Gulf Coast. *Wikipedia.*

became independent countries from Spain. There was also considerable infighting between various groups in Mexico over who would be in charge of their country.

The U.S. Navy threatened Lafitte and his pirates due to attacks on U.S. shipping and attacks in American waters. Lafitte left Campeachy in 1821 after burning down Maison Rouge. There are many different stories about how and where Jean Lafitte died. He likely died off Honduras in 1823 after attacking Spanish vessels. Legends of Lafitte's lost treasure in Texas include Calhoun, Cameron, Chambers, Galveston, Harris, Jackson, Jefferson, Kenedy, Kleberg, Matagorda, Nueces, Orange, Rusk, Victoria and Willacy Counties. There are also many areas in Louisiana with Lafitte's lost treasure mentioned in legends.

Chapter 8

SHIPWRECKS

*T*exas has a long coastline with the Gulf of Mexico and is subject
to the wrath of hurricanes and fierce storms, which have claimed a
large number of ships. Many ships have disappeared in the Gulf of
Mexico off the Texas coast, from Spanish colonial days up to the advent of
modern communication. The Texas state marine archaeologist has almost
two thousand shipwrecks on the Texas shipwrecks registry. One of the first
recorded shipwrecks was in 1528, when Cabeza de Vaca and his crew were
shipwrecked on Galveston Island as survivors of Pineda's Florida expedition.

The French ship *La Belle* was wrecked in Matagorda Bay in 1686 and
located in 1995. It was part of Rene-Robert Cavelier, Sieur de La Salle's
attempt to claim Texas for France and establish French colonies there.
La Belle was excavated and is now part of an exhibit in the Bullock Texas
History Museum in Austin, as well as other museums.

During the Mexican War, several ships sank in the Brazos Santiago Pass
and other sites in or near the Rio Grande. Some of shipwrecks in Cameron
County carried specie, which may or may not have been recovered.

During the American Civil War, at least eighty warships, blockade runners
and coastal vessels were lost due to battles, storms, bad navigation and other
causes. Treasure may be associated with some of these shipwrecks, especially
blockade runners. The 1875 Indianola hurricane sank a number of ships
along the Texas Gulf Coast between Galveston and Matamoros, Mexico.
Some of these ships carried specie and bullion.

USS *Westfield* blows up in Galveston Bay during the Civil War. *U.S. Naval History and Heritage Command.*

Ships that sank with no loss of life would generally not have treasure aboard when they sank, as there was likely enough time to remove it before the vessel went underwater. Many vessels were stranded entering or leaving Texas coastal ports before dredging opened regular ship channels. Shifting sands due to the mighty rivers dropping sediment, in additional to the coastal Gulf of Mexico currents, claimed many vessels in the Brazos Santiago and Matamoros area as well as elsewhere. The shipwrecks noted in this book have only had a minimal amount of research done into them. Salvage of their specie and cargo or even raising of the wrecks was likely done for some of these shipwrecks.

BIBLIOGRAPHY

Books

Arnold, J. Barto, III. *Marine Magnetometer Survey of Archeological Materials Found Near Galveston, Texas*. Publication No. 10. Austin: Texas Antiquities Committee, 1987.

Baer, Dr. Robert H. *Texas Treasure: Billy Kenon and the Padre Island, Shipwrecks of 1554*. Merritt Island, FL: Signum Ops, 2020.

Caran, Christopher, Joe R. Wallace, and James Stotts. *Geology and Historical Mining, Llano Uplift Region, Central Texas*. Guidebook 20. Austin, TX: Austin Geological Society, 2000.

Clark, Howard D. *Lost Mines of the Old West*. Buena Park, CA: Ghost Town Press, 1951.

Cumberland, Charles C. *Mexico, The Struggle for Modernity*. Oxford University Press, 1973.

Daly, Loraine, and Pat Reumert. *The Padre Island Story*. San Antonio, TX: Naylor, 1966.

Dobie, J. Frank. *Coronado's Children: Tales of Lost Mines and Buried Treasures of the Southwest*. Austin: University of Texas Press, 1978.

———, ed. *Legends of Texas: Lost Mines and Buried Treasure*. Vol. 1. Gretna, LA: Pelican Publishing: 1975.

———. *Legends of Texas: Pirates' Gold and Other Tales*. Vol. 2. Gretna, LA: Pelican Publishing: 2012.

Drago, Henry Sinclair. *Lost Bonanzas*. New York: Pocket Books, 1967.

Gaines, W. Craig. *Civil War Gold and Other Lost Treasure: Revised Edition*. Privately published: Amazon, 2017.

———. *Hispanic Lost Treasures of the Eastern U.S.* Privately published: Amazon, 2019.

———. *Lost Oklahoma Treasure*. Charleston, SC: The History Press, 2021.

Gwynne, S.C. *Empire of the Summer Moon: Quanah Parker and the Rise and Fall of the Comanches, the Most Powerful Indian Tribe in American History*. New York: Scribner, 2010.

Hart, Herbert M. *Old Forts of the Far West*. New York: Bonanza Books, 1965.

Haydock, Tim. *Treasure Trove: Where to Find the Greatest Lost Treasures of the World*. New York: Henry Holt, 1986.

Henson, Michael Paul. *America's Lost Treasures*. South Bend, IN: Jayco, 1984.

Jameson, W.C. *Buried Treasures of the American Southwest*. Little Rock, AR: August House, 1989.

———. *Buried Treasures of Texas*. Little Rock, AR: August House, 1991.

———. *Treasure Hunter: A Memoir of Caches, Curses, and Confrontation*. Lanham, MD: Taylor Trade, 2014.

Lardas, Mark. *The Vanished Texas Coast*. Charleston, SC: The History Press, 2021.

Lewis, David C. *The San Saba Treasure: Legends of Silver Creek*. Denton: University of North Texas, 2018.

Lytle, William M., and Forrest R. Holdcamper. *Merchant Steam Vessels of the United States, 1790–1868*. Revised and edited by C. Bradford Mitchell and Kenneth R. Hall. Staten Island, NY: Steamship Historical Society of America, 1975.

Marx, Robert F. *Buried Treasure of the United States*. New York: Bonanza Books, 1980.

———. *Shipwrecks of the Americas*. New York: Dover, 1987.

——— and Jennifer Marx. *The Search for Sunken Treasure: Exploring the World's Lost Shipwrecks*. Toronto, ON: Key Porter Books, 1996.

Mayo, Nancy Ellen. *The Archaeology and History of Spanish Colonial Mining Efforts in Central Texas*. Master's thesis, Texas Tech University, 1995.

Nesmith, Robert I., and John S. Potter Jr. *Treasure: How and Where to Find It*. New York: Arco, 1968.

Patterson, Richard. *Historical Atlas of the Outlaw West*. Boulder, CO: Johnson Books, 1993.

Penfield, Thomas. *Buried Treasure in the U.S. and Where to Find It*. New York: Grosset & Dunlap, 1969.

———. *Dig Here!* San Antonio, TX: Naylor, 1971.

———. *A Guide to Treasure in Texas*. Conroe, TX: True Treasure Library, 1972.

Potter, John S., Jr. *The Treasure Diver's Guide*. Garden City, NY: Doubleday, 1960.

Schurmacher, Emile C. *Lost Treasures and How to Find Them!* New York: Paperback Library, 1968.

Steiger, Brad. *Treasure Hunting*. New York: Ace Books, 1967.

Terry, Thomas P. *United States Treasure Map Atlas*. La Crosse, WI: Specialty Products, 1981.

Throckmorton, Peter, ed. *The Sea Remembers: Shipwrecks and Archaeology*. New York: Smithmark, 1987.

Triplett, Frank. *The Life, Times and Treacherous Death of Jesse James*. 1882; repr., Stamford: Connecticut Swallow Press, 1992.

Wilson, Steve. *Oklahoma Treasures and Treasure Tales*. Norman: University of Oklahoma Press, 1976.

———. *The Spider Rock Treasure: A Texas Mystery of Lost Spanish Gold*. Fort Worth, TX: Eakin Press, 2004.

Articles

Aldridge, Jim. "Pancho Villa's Texas Hoard." *True Treasure* 7, no. 4 (March–April 1973): 45.

Alley, H.L. "Outlaw Treasure and Spanish Gold, Spanish Fort." *Artifact*, July 1967, 6–8.

———. "Outlaw Treasure and Spanish Gold, Spanish Fort, A Tale of Texas Treasure and a Search That Uncovered Part of It." *Treasure* 1, no. 6 (April 1971): 57.

Anderson, Eugene. "Hidden Gold of the Guadalupes." *True Treasure* 6, no. 2 (January–February 1972): 28–31.

———. "Maximilian's Treasure—Fact or Fantasy?" *Treasure World* 4, no. 27 (June–July 1970): 54–60, 62–64.

———. "Missing Cache of the James Brothers." *True Treasure* 9, no. 6 (May–June 1975): 12–15.

———. "The Missing Mine of the Mission San Saba." *Western Treasures* 5, no. 4 (August 1970): 12–17.

Arnold, J. Barto, III, and Melinda Arceneaux Wickman. "Padre Island Spanish Shipwrecks of 1554." Texas State Historical Association. Originally published 1976; last updated October 29, 2021. https://www.tshaonline. org/handbook/entries/padre-island-spanish-shipwrecks-of-1554.

Atchley, D. Van. "$18,000 Buried at Old Fort Belknap." *Treasure World* 9, no. 3 (February–March 1975): 32.

————. "Buried Gold Cache." *Lost Treasure* 2, no. 9 (August 1977): 26.

Atchley, Danny. "Blue Hills Treasure." *Treasure Cache 2003 Annual*, 17–18.

Boren, Kerry Ross. "Red River Treasure." *Treasure World* 9, no. 9 (August–September 1975): 40.

Carson, Xanthus. "Has the San Saba Silver Mine Been Found?" *Treasure World* 8, no. 11 (October–November 1970): 40–42, 47–50.

————. "Karl Steinheimer's Lost Millions Are Real." *Treasure* 7, no. 9 (September 1976): 70–76.

————. "Pancho Villa's Missing Millions." *Treasure World* 6, no. 3 (February–March 1972): 15–16, 18–20.

Carter, Sharon. "Bob Herring's Lost Gold." *Lost Treasure* 28, no. 3 (March 2004): 19–20.

Conant, Lora M. "Lost Cache of $20 Gold Coins." *True Treasure* 5, no. 4 (March–April 1971): 62–64.

Concoles, Trini. "Lost Bandit's Loot in Texas." *Lost Treasure* 33, no. 8 (August 2008): 10.

Davenport, R.N., and J.M. Forker. "The Elusive Lost Santa Saba Mine." *True Treasure*, 8 no. 2 (January–February 1974): 65–67.

Dearmore, B.F. "Spanish Fort Treasure." *Old West* 11, no. 4 (Fall 1975): 39.

De Morest, Elizabeth Marie. "The Last Laugh, Lost Sublett Gold Mine." *Treasure Cache 1999*: 28–30.

Dobie, J. Frank. "A Startling Theory on How Jim Bowie Got His Silver." *Gold!* 2, no. 1 Annual (1970): 29, 66.

Eckhardt, C.F. "A Strange Story of Pirate Treasure Along the Texas Gulf Coast." *Treasure Search* 14, no. 6 (November–December 1986): 44–46.

Eckhart, Jerry. "Where The Buffalo Roam, Gold Stacked Like Cordwood." *Treasure Cache 2000*: 74–75.

Escuriex, Jalon. "The Saga of San Saba." *Treasure World* 6, no. 11 (October–November 1972): 40–41, 48–49.

Ferguson, Jeff. "Texas Navy's Missing Silver Bars." *True Treasure* 9, no. 10 (September–October 1975): 16–19.

Ferguson, Robert G. "Camp-Fire Tales of Lost Mines and Hidden Treasure." *Gold!* 3, no. 3 (Summer 1971): 63–65, 70–71.

Finger, Herb. "Hooker's Cave." *National Treasure Hunters League* no. 2 (Summer 1969): 20.

Fischer, Jon. "Lost Slave Gold in Texas." *True Treasure* 8, no. 12 (November–December 1974): 43.

Gaines, W. Craig. "The Lost San Saba Mines." *Lost Treasure* 40, no. 7 (July 2015): 48–49.

———. "Shifting Sands and Offshore Waters." *Treasure Cache 2000 Annual*: 50–54.

———. "Where's Lafitte's Loot Buried?" *Lost Treasure* 24, no. 12 (December 1999): 8–9.

———. "Who Owns the Shipwreck?" *Treasure Facts 2003*: 9–10.

Garrett, David E. "Spanish Trails and San Saba Legends." *World of Treasures* 6, no. 2 (June 1981): 24–25, 28.

Getz, Donald E. "The Meanest Santa Claus Cache." *Treasure World* 6, no. 11 (October–November 1972): 35–36, 41.

Hale, Duane, and Robert Kyker. "The San Saba Mines, Part I." *Treasure* 22, no. 3 (March 1991): 58–64.

———. "The San Saba Mines, Part II." *Treasure* 22, no. 4 (April 1991): 62–67, 79–80.

———. "The San Saba Mines, Part III." *Treasure* 22, no. 5 (May 1991): 14–15, 26, 47, 78–81, 85.

———. "The San Saba Mines, Part IV." *Treasure* 22, no. 6 (June 1991): 64–69, 78–81, 83.

Hamilton, Carter B. "Flower Hamilton's Money." *Treasure World* 3, no. 2 (June–July 1969): 37–38.

Hamilton, George B. "Lost Texas Lead Mine." *Treasure World* 5, no. 5 (April–May 1971): 59–60.

Hathcock, Steve. "Charles Hardin's Amazing Find." *Treasure Cache 2004*: 32–34.

Henderson, Jeff W. "Does the Castle Gap Treasure Really Exist?" *Treasure World* 8, no. 1 (December–January 1975): 26–29.

———. "Treasure at Castle Gap." *True Treasure* 5, no. 4 (March–April 1971): 36–38.

Henson, Michael Paul. "Treasures New and Old Lie under Texas Soil." *Lost Treasure* 9, no. 12 (December 1984): 46–48.

Highley, J. Scott. "Resaca de la Palma's Missing Treasure." *True Treasure* 6, no. 2 (January–February 1972): 46–48.

Hudson, Steve. "The Famous Lafitte Was amongst Them." *Lost Treasure* 10, no. 7 (July 1985): 14–16.

Hughes, Pat. "Aztec Treasure: Does It Still Exist?" *Lost Treasure* 30, no. 9 (September 2005): 47–48.

Hutton, Kenneth. "Relics Aplenty on the Texas Coast." *Western Treasures* 4, no. 1 (October 1968): 14–19.

Ingle, Fletcher. "Texas Fortune." *Best of Western Treasures Annual 1970*: 26–27.

Jameson, W.C. "Shafter Lake's Incredible Lost Treasure." *Lost Treasure* 19, no. 8 (August 1994): 39–41.

Kelly, Bill. "Bulk of $79,000 Still Missing." *Treasure Search* 10, no. 4 (August 1982): 56–60, 66.

Kutac, C. "Treasure in Hendricks Lake." *Treasure World* 9, no. 21 (December–January 1975): 64, 66.

Lasco, Jack. "Still Buried in Texas, Emperor Maximilian's $5 Million Treasure." *Saga's Treasure Special* 1, no. 1 (1970): 25–27, 70–72, 74.

Masters, John A. "Does the Lost San Saba Mine Really Exist?" *Gold!* 1, no. 1 Annual (1969): 94–96.

Mikhailoff, Byron Lee. "Rock Pens Treasure." *Treasure World* 7, no. 3 (March 1973): 27.

Mullings, Willie. "Lost Gold on Bad Luck Creek." *Treasure World* 7, no. 7 (June–July 1973): 59.

Nelson, George. "Texas." *Lost Treasure* 42, no. 11 (November 2017): 50–53.

Pallante, Anthony J. "Texas: Legendary Lost Mines." *Lost Treasure* 4, no. 12 (December 1999): 43–46.

———. "Texas: Seminole Bill." *Lost Treasure* 26, no. 4 (April 2001): 39–42.

Ray, Richard. "Missing Safe." *Lost Treasure* 1, no. 1 (December 1975): 33.

Reid, Sheila. "Silver Decoy, Lost Train Robber's Loot at Big Bend, Texas." *Treasure Cache 2002*: 77–80.

Rountree, J.G. "Lost Gold on the Rio Grande." *True Treasure* 5, no. 6 (May–June 1971): 20–26.

———. "Lost Silver Ledge." *Treasure World* 5, no. 3 (February–March 1971): 36, 41.

———. "Perils of Padre Island." *True Treasure* 3, no. 4 (July–August 1969): 40–46.

Rutherford, Phillip R. "The Rabbit Hole Full of Gold." *Treasure Search* 11, no. 2 (April 1983): 46–48.

Santleben, August. "Looting the Freight Haulers in Texas." *Gold!* Whole no. 9 (Winter 1974), 22–23, 45–46.

Shriver, John P. "Lost Mule Pen Cache." *Treasure World* 8, no. 3 (February–March 1974): 24.

Sweatt, Marcus. "Lost Chisos Mine." *True Treasure* 3, no. 14 (October–November 1969): 50.

———. "Lost Gold in the Big Bend." *True Treasure* 4, no. 12 (November–December 1970): 63–64.

"Treasure at Horsehead Crossing." *True Treasure* 3, no. 6 (November–December 1969): 24.

"Treasure in the News, Court Battle of Texas Treasure Ownership." *Treasure* 1, no. 4 (December 1970): 16.

Vance, Tom. "Red River Treasures." *Lost Treasure* 31, no. 9 (September 2006): 15–17.

———. "Texas: Copper Pots Full of Coins amongst the Stash." *Lost Treasure* 27, no. 8 (August 2002): 40–42.

Villa, Benito. "Buried Near Paris, Texas." *Lost Treasure* 2, no. 7 (June 1977): 25–26.

Wagner, Ken. "Bonanza of the Old Texas Trails." In "True Frontier Special No. 12." Special issue, *Treasure*, (Spring 1975): 30–35, 62–63.

Watkins, Clara. "Spanish Bullion." *Treasure Cache 2004*: 40–42.

Weeks, Dave. "Closing In on Lafitte's Treasure." *Treasure Search* 6, no. 4 (August 1978): 8–10, 46.

Wilson, Steve. "Cryptic Copper Plates—Clues to a Spanish Treasure?" *True Treasure* 5, no. 12 (December 1971): 58–64.

———. "Endless Quest for the Spider Rock Treasure, Part I." *Treasure World* 6, no. 8 (July–August 1972): 38–42, 47.

———. "Endless Quest for the Spider Rock Treasure, Part II." *Treasure World* 6, no. 9 (August–September 1972): 40–42, 50–52.

———. "Missing Spanish Treasure Near Double Mountain." *True Treasure* 6, no. 4 (March–April 1972): 34–38, 43.

Zehner, Chuck. "Nolan's Lost Gold." *Lost Treasure* 1, no. 12 (November 1976): 15–17.

Websites: Various Articles

Legends of America. www.legendsofamerica.com.

Texas Historical Commission. www.thc.texas.gov.

Texas State Historical Association. "Handbook of Texas." www.tshaonline.org/handbook.

The Portal to Texas History. www.texashistory.unt.edu.

Wikipedia. www.wikipedia.org.

INDEX

A

Abilene 32, 53, 131
Acapulco, Mexico 152
Adamsville 45, 81
Aguayo, Marquis de Miguel de 14
Aguilares (Eagle's Nest) 145
Alamo 16, 17, 100, 157, 160, 191
Alamo Canyon 32
Alamocito Creek 111
Albany 126
Alice Sadell (ship) 41
Allamoore 69, 154
Alley, H.L. 104
Alpine 24
Alta Loma Mountain 97
Alvin 20
Ana Cacho (Anacacho) Mountains 79
Anahuac 43
Anderson, Eugene R. (author) 47
Apache Canyon 47
Apaches 68, 69, 70, 89, 114, 155
Apple Springs 135
Aransas Creek 14
Aransas Pass 10, 110, 122
Archer City 11
Arista, General Mariano 32, 36, 161

Arkansas River 111
Armstrong 77, 117
Arnold, Dave 32, 129
Artesia Wells 83
Aspermont 128, 129, 130
Atascosa River 87
Attoyac Bayou 106
Attoyac River 122
Aury, Louis-Michel 164
Austin 14, 15, 89, 93, 133, 134, 163, 166
Austin Geological Society 90
Austin, Stephen F. 59
Austin (Texas sloop) 38
Austwell 120
Avery 118
Aztec 66, 95, 119, 128, 141, 155

B

Bad Luck Creek 114
Baffin Bay 77, 80
Bagdad, Mexico 36
Baird 126
Balli (or Belli), Padre Nicolas 41
Bandera Pass 78
Banks, Major General Nathaniel 39

Barataria Bay, Louisiana 164
Barber's Hill 57
Barney, Ben 85
Barney, Ella 85
Barrel Spring 73
Bass Gang 51, 112, 163
Bass, Sam 25, 28, 45, 49, 50, 51, 71,
    91, 104, 112, 128, 133, 148,
    149, 163
Battle Branch 67
Battle Creek 67
Battle of New Orleans, Louisiana 164
Battle of Palo Alto 36, 161
Battle of Resaca de la Palma 32, 33,
    161
Battle of San Jacinto 30, 64, 72, 135
Battle of the Two Villages 158
Bay Ridge 63
Bayside 120
Bean, Ellis 67
Beasley (man) 123
Beef Creek 121
Beeville 13, 14
Belton 15
Belt's Ferry 135
Belt, William T. 135
Benbrook 130
Benbrook Lake 131
Benuit, Joni 94
Bertillion, L.D. (author) 15
Bewley, Captain 96
Big Bend National Park 21, 22, 23, 24,
    25, 26
Big Caddo Creek 128
Big Lake 137
Big Sandy Creek 84
Big Spring 68, 139
Big Springs, Nebraska 51, 112, 163
Big Thicket 85
Black Rock Peak 23
Black Springs 71
Blanco (man) 90
Blanco River 90
Blooming Grove 107

Bois D'Arc Crossing 70
Bolivar Point 59
Boone's Ferry 135
Boonville 21
Boquillas, Mexico 22, 26
Borger 70
Bouce, Rube 91
Bowie 104
Bowie Creek 85, 86
Bowie, Jim 100, 102, 160
Bowie, Rezin 100
Brazos Bar 34, 39
Brazos Island 34, 35, 37, 39
Brazos River 19, 20, 21, 95, 128, 158
Brazos Santiago Pass 34, 37, 166
Breckinridge 127, 128
Bremond 86
Bridgeport 149
Brinson, Enoch 63
Brinson's Point 63
Bronte 44
Brookeland 121
Brownsville 13, 32, 35, 36, 37, 77, 159
Brownwood 27
Buck Creek 124
Buena Vista Plantation 143
Buffalo Bayou 62, 64, 160
Buffalo Gap 131
Bugantine (Bergantin, Brigatine) Creek
    120
Bullis Bend 26
Bullis Crossing 144
Bullock Texas History Museum 166
Burnet 28
Burnet-San Saba Crossing 28
Burton, Wes 134
Butler, Reese 93

C

Caddo 65, 157
Caddo Lake 65
Caesar (man) 67
Caja Mountain 97

Calamity Creek 23
Caldwell 27
Calf Creek 96, 100
Calf Creek (town) 96
Callaway, Luke 79
Cambren family 70
Campbell, Jim 19
Campbell's Bayou 19
Campeachy 164, 165
Camp Freeman 106
Camp Wood 118
Canadian River 111
Cariza Pass 114
Carlsbad, New Mexico 48, 49
Carrie A. Thomas (ship) 127
Carrizo Springs 52
Carson City, Nevada 117
Carson, Xanthus (author) 16
Carter, Bellas 150
Carter, Will 137
Casa Blanca 75, 87, 108
Casner brothers 116
Casner, John 116
Cassidy (man) 95
Castell 90, 91
Castle Gap 109, 136, 138, 139
Cedar Bayou 62
Cedar Gap Mountain 131
Cedar Mountain 91
Center Point 78
Cerro del Almagre 90
Chalk Hill 49, 50
Chapman, Henry 112
Cherokees 136
Chief Geronimo 68, 69
Chief Lone Wolf 104
Chief Santana (Satanta) 44
Chief Victorio 69
Chief Yellow Wolf 7, 88, 144
Chihuahua, Mexico 23, 67
Chihuahua Trail 76, 155
Chisos Mountains 21, 22, 23
Chocolate Bayou 19
Christoval 133

Cibalo Creek 114
Cinenia 79
Cisco 32, 53
Civilian Conservation Corps 112
Civil War 9, 19, 36, 41, 63, 64, 80,
    103, 118, 129, 138, 151, 166
Clark, Howard (author) 49
Clear Fork Creek 28, 112
Clear Fork of the Brazos River 126
Clyde 32, 33
Coahuila 83
Collins Creek 126
Colonel Harvey (ship) 34
Colonel Rufus (ship) 20
Colonel Yell (ship) 122
Colorado River 28, 44, 88, 90, 94,
    123, 125, 134, 155
Columbia (ship) 34
Columbus, New Mexico 159
Comancheros 70
Comanches 7, 9, 12, 28, 70, 81, 87,
    88, 96, 106, 118, 124, 138, 140,
    144, 148, 155, 156, 157, 158
Coma Ranch 14
Commerce 67
Compton, Bert 137
Comstock 142
Concho River 132, 133
Constitution (ship) 29
Copano Bay 119, 120
Corpus Christi 37, 108, 109, 110, 119
Corpus Christi Bay 76, 109, 122, 138
Corpus Christi Museum of Science
    and History 147, 153
Corrigan 10
Corsicana 107
Cortez, Hernando 87
Cortina, Juan Nepomuceno 35, 159
Cortina War 159
Cos, General 97
Cotulla 83
Cove Hollow 45
Cox Creek 72
Crane 46

Crawford 96
Cremony, Major John C. 69
Criss, L.C. 55
Croton Creek 51, 79
Crystal City 52

D

Dagger Hollow 134
Daily, L.J. 65
Dallas 49, 50, 60, 76, 163
Dalton, Bill 61
Dalton, M.L. 111
Davis Mountains 73, 118
Dawson, Robert 121
Dayton 85, 86
Dead Man's Lake 62
Decatur 149
De Gavilan, Captain 48, 49
Del Rio 141, 142
Denton 50, 51, 104
Devil's Den 149
Devil's River 141, 142
Dexter 45, 105
Diboll 10
Dickens 51
Dickens Hill 51
Dinero 87
Dobie, J. Frank (author) 8, 12, 16, 57,
    69, 87, 134
Dobie, Sterling 123
Dodge Cattle Trail 93
Dondolo (Austrian ship) 138
Dorso 142
Double Mountain 128, 129
Double Mountain Fork of the Brazos
    River 128, 129
Double Mountains 129
Drago, Harry Sinclair (author) 90, 100
Dripping Springs 65
Driscoll 108
Dryden 131
Duck Creek 50
Duke, Andy K. 150

Dunham, Dan 97
Duran, Jesse 48

E

Eagle Ford 69
Eagle Mountains 69
Eagle Pass 95
E.A. Ogden (ship) 20
East Fork of the Trinity River 50
Edroy 122
1818 hurricane 58
1886 hurricane 30
1875 hurricane 20, 30, 35, 166
El Camino Real 87
Elephant Mountain 23
El Fortin 87
El Fortin de Cibolo 115
Elm Pass 78
El Muerto Springs 73
El Nuevo Constante (Spanish ship) 58
El Paso 54, 55, 56, 69, 137, 154, 157,
    159
El Paso del Norte, Mexico 54, 157
Emory Peak 21
Emperor Maximilian 109, 113, 114,
    137, 138, 139
Emperor Napoleon III 137
English 118
Epley Springs 103
E.P. Wright (ship) 34
Espantosa Lake (Ghostly Lake,
    Horrible Lake) 52
Espiritu Santo (Spanish ship) 146, 153
Estambel Hill 82
Estrada, Juan 73
Evant 45

F

False Live Oak Point 10, 29
Fannin, Colonel James 160
1554 fleet 146, 147, 153
1552 fleet 39

Filisola, General Vincente 145
Fisk, Earl 137
Flagpole Hill Park 50
Flint, John 46
Flores, Captain Palacio 52
Flour Bluff 109
Flying H Bar Ranch 32
Fogg, John "Old Man" 108
Ford, Robert 163
Fort Belknap 150
Fort Colorado (Fort Prairie) 133
Fort Concho 132
Fort Croghan 28, 148
Fort Davis 73, 74, 115
Fort Elliott 146
Fort Ewell 82, 98
Fort Griffin 126
Fort Hudson 142
Fort McKavett 78
Fort Merrill 87
Fort Planticlan 108
Fort Ramirez 87
Fort Sill, Oklahoma 44, 68
Fort Stockton 69, 113
Fort Teran 135
Fort Worth 112, 130, 131, 163
49ers 11, 131, 144
Fowlerton 98
Franklin Mountains 54, 55
Freeport 20
Frio Canyon 118, 140
Frio Draw 111
Frio River 87, 118, 140
Frio Town 95
Frontier (ship) 34
Frost 107
Furman, Harold 28

G

Galveston 39, 42, 49, 60, 166
Galveston Bay 43, 59, 164
Galveston Island 19, 30, 57, 58, 59, 60,
    152, 164, 166

Galvez Town 164
Gamel, John W. 93
Garcitas Creek 72
Garland 50
Genoa, Nevada 118
George Griffis Ranch 66
George West 87
Gholson's Gap 45
Giddings 84
Gilmer 136
Gilpin 51
Globe (ship) 35
Goacher, James 84
Gold Point 94
Goldthwaite 103
Goliad 87, 108, 160
Gonzales, Dario 145
Gonzales (man) 106
Gonzales, Policarpo 69
Goodnight, Charles 71, 117
Grachias, Jesus Ramon 117
Graham, Marion 86
Grapeshot (ship) 59
Grapevine Springs 47
Gray, Mayberry "Mustang" 108
Green, Pronto 141
Greenville 70
Guadalupe Mountains 47, 48, 49, 68,
    69
Guadalupe Mountains National Park
    47, 48
Guadalupe Peak 49
Guadalupe River 143
Guerra (friend) 15

H

Halfway Hill 85
Hall, Eli 114
Halletsville 84
Hamilton 45
Hamilton, Flower 121
Hamilton, George B. (author) 73
Hamlin (farmer) 134

Hardin, Charles 41
Harmon, Buck 27
Hart, Will 137
Hasinai 12, 157
Helena 76
Henderson, Jeff W. (author) 139
Hendricks Lake 120
Henry, O. 134
Hext 99
Hickory Creek 51
Higgin 66
Hightower, John 86
Hill (man) 30
Hillsboro 66
Hoffman (man) 139
Honey Creek 90, 155
Hooker, Robert 66
Hooker's Cave 66
Horsehead Crossing 113, 137, 138
Horse Mountain 22
Hot Springs 22
Houston 63, 160
Houston, Sam 160
Hubbard Creek 126, 128
Hughes (railroad engineer) 24
Humble 62
Huntsville Prison Cemetery 44
Hurricane Beulah 146

I

Ida Lewis (ship) 35
Inca 128, 155
Independence Creek 132
Independence (ship) 29
Indian Hot Springs 70
Indianola 30, 166
Indian Territory 60, 68, 81, 141

J

Jacksboro 70, 71
Jackson (cowboy) 150
Jackson, Mose 103

James, Frank 47, 113, 162, 163
James, Jesse 47, 49, 60, 87, 95, 113,
        162, 163
Jameson, W.C. (author) 47, 69
Jamison, Henry 138
Jessie (ship) 35
Jim Hughes–Curly Bill Gang 73
Jim Ned Settlement 27
Joe White's Cave 107
John's Creek 65
Johnson, Dr. John M. 84
Johnson, Mrs. 85
Jones, Wallace 137
Juarez, Pablo 15
Juarez Point, Mexico 38
Juaristas 114, 137, 139
Juniper Canyon 22
Juniper Springs 48
Juno 142

K

Kansas City 111
Kate, Gamel 93
Katy 143
Kelly, Bill (Seminole Bill) 26, 27
Kenefik (Kennifluk) 85
Kenon, Billy 153
Kermit 148
Key, Mrs. 99
Key, Watt 99
Kiamichi Mountains, Oklahoma 141
King Ranch 123
Kingsland 90, 91
Kiowa 44, 66, 104
Kirkpatrick, Dr. James 103
Knight, Tom 137
Kosse 86

L

La Belle (French ship) 166
La Caraquena (*Guipuzcuana*) (Spanish
        ship) 59

La Esmeralda 54
Lafitte, Jean 19, 30, 31, 37, 43, 59, 63, 72, 74, 80, 94, 109, 111, 120, 153, 164, 165
Lafitte's Grove 59, 60
Lagarto 86, 88
Laguna Madre 41, 109
Lake Charlotte 64
Lake Corpus Christi 88, 108
Lake Dallas 50
Lake Garza-Little 50
Lake Lewisville 50
Lake Miller 43
Lake Sam Rayburn 121
Lake Texoma 60
Lake Wichita 11
Lampasas River 15
La Porte 63
La Pryor 151
L'Archeveque, Sostenes 117
Laredo 52, 87, 98, 145
Laredo Crossing 76
Laredo–San Antonio Crossing 82
La Salle, Sieur de 166
Las Chuzas Mountains 97
Lassiter, Sourdough 108
Lavaca Bay 30, 72
Lavaca River 30, 72, 84
Leach, James B. 54
Leach, Walter 129
lead 51, 65, 72, 73, 79, 84, 85, 91, 101, 118, 121, 139, 149, 154
Leakey 118
Leander 147
Lea (ship) 35
Leon, Alonso de 157
Leon River 15
Lewis, David C. (author) 90
Liberty 85
Lighthouse Canyon 117
Lipan Apaches 12
Lipantitlan 76
Little Cypress Creek 136
Little Fleeta (ship) 42

Little Fort 87
Little Llano River 89
Little River 14
Little Wichita River 71
Lively (ship) 59
Liverpool 19
Llano 91
Llano River 88, 89, 90, 93, 100, 124, 155
Llano Uplift 154
Lockhart 28, 29
Loflin, Ben 66
Lolita 72
Loma Alta 141
Lometa 82
London 88
Lone Oak Bayou 43
Lone Wolf Mountain 104
Longest, Thomas 79
Longhorn Cavern 28
Long Island 36
Long, James 59
Longview 61
Lopez, Antonio 77
Lopez, Padre 104
Lordsburg 48
Los Mina de las Almagres 89
Los Moros 140
Los Moros Creek 79
Lost City 36, 41
Lost Lake 43
Lost Mine Peak 22
Lost Mine Trail 22
Low, William 67
Loyas Ranch Settlement 145
Lufkin 10
Luing 29
Lynchburg 62

M

Mansfield Channel 147
Mansfield Cut 153

Mansfield Cut Underwater
    Archeological District 146, 147,
    153
Maravillas River (Creek) 22, 23
Marfa 24, 116
Maria Theresa (French ship) 42
Marshall 64, 65
Martin 55
Martin Creek 121
Martinez, Colas 117
Marx, Robert (author) 8
Mason 93
Mason family 70
Matagorda Bay 29, 30, 31, 120, 166
Matamoros, Mexico 35, 166
Mathis 123
Mayo, Nancy Ellen 90
McDougal Creek 102
McFarland, Samuel Lewis 28
McGaffey, Neil 74, 75
McGloin's Bluff 122
McKim Creek 121
McKim Hills 72
McKinney (helper) 55
McKittrick Canyon 47
McNeal brothers 95
McNeil 133
Mecerno, Captain Francisco del 146,
    153
Menard 78, 89, 90, 93, 96, 100, 102,
    124, 125, 155
Mesquiteville 70
Mexican War 32, 34, 57, 122, 159,
    161, 166
Mexico City 48, 52, 161
Mexico (ship) 37
Middle Alamoso Creek 111
Middle Concho River 70, 132
Mikeska 87
Miller, U.S. Marshall Henry 81
Miranda y Flores, Don Bernardo de
    89, 155
Mission Nuestra Senora del Guadalupe
    54

Mission San Antonio de Valero 16
Mission San Gabriel 102
Mission San Lorenzo 118
Mission San Saba 100, 101, 155, 157,
    171
Mission Santa Cruz de San Saba 12,
    101, 155
Mission San Vincente 22
Mobeetee 145
Monahans 144
Money Hill (Nueces County) 110
Money Hill (Padre Island) 41
Money Hill (Tyler County) 136
Money Hole 86
Monterrey, Mexico 73, 150
Montezuma 119, 141, 147
Moore, Deputy Sheriff Maurice 163
Morgan's Point 63
Moro (Spaniard) 143
Mount Bonnel 133
Mud Creek 141
Mullin 103
Murphy, Jed 85
Murphy, Jim 163
Murphyville 24
Musgraves (man) 83
Musquiz, Lieutenant Miguel 67
Mustang Creek 67
Mustang Island 109, 110

N

Nacogdoches 67, 106, 122, 135
Nacona 104
Nard, William or Bill 91
Natchez, Mississippi 67
Naughton, Paul 137
Navasota River 135
Neches River 72, 74, 135, 136
New Orleans, Louisiana 30, 75, 99,
    107
Newton Brothers 18
Newton Gang 18, 163
Newton, Jess (Joseph) 18

Nolan Creek 67
Nolan, Phillip 67
Nolan River 67
North Beach 110
North Concho River 132
North Croton Creek 79
North Llano River 88
Nueces Flats 14
Nueces River 10, 18, 19, 82, 83, 87, 88, 97, 98, 108, 109, 118, 122, 151, 161
Nueces Strip 161

O

Oakville 88
Obregon, President Alvaro 159
Odessa 49
Ojo de Agua Ramirena Rancho 87
Old River 85
Olmos 14
Olmos Pass 12
Olmsted, Frank D. 129
Onion Creek 66, 96
Oppencoffer, Fred 110
Ordones, Benito 24
Ortega, Manuel 23
Oso Creek 110
Outlaw, Bass 46
Oxford 91
Ozona 25, 46
Ozosi, Captain Alonso 153

P

Pacer, Dirk 141
Packsaddle Mountain (Brewster County) 25, 27
Packsaddle Mountain (Llano County) 90, 91
Padre Island 8, 34, 36, 37, 38, 39, 40, 41, 42, 80, 146, 147, 153
Padre Island National Seashore Park 42, 153

Paisano Pass 24
Paisano (ship) 42
Palmer Lake 80
Palmetto (ship) 30
Palo Duro Canyon 117
Palo Duro State Park 117
Palo Pinto Canyon 116
Paris 80
Parrilla, Colonel Diego Ortiz 157
Paso Piedra 108, 109
Paso Valeno 87
Pecan Bayou 103
Pecos 119
Pecos River 113, 119, 132, 136, 137, 138, 141, 142, 144, 150
Pegleg Crossing 102
Pelican Island 58, 60
Pena Creek 52
Penfield, Thomas (author) 8, 32, 73, 129
Perry, Harp 124
Philadelphia (ship) 10
Phillips, Robert Lee 137
Pilot Point 51
Pine Canyon 23
Pine Creek 80
Piney Point 63
Pinto Canyon 74
Pizzaro, Francisco 128
Platoro Limited Inc. 146, 153
Pleasanton 12
Point of Rocks 80
Pond Creek 45
Pontoon Crossing 113
Port Arthur 75
Porter, William Sydney 134
Port Isabel 37, 39, 41
Port Neches 74
Potter, John S., Jr. (author) 42, 109, 138
Pottsboro 60
Presidio 116
Presidio Crossing 18, 19
Presidio de San Luis de las Amarillas 12, 155

Presidio de San Vincente 22
Presidio La Bahia 160
Presidio Mine 154
Pride (ship) 43, 63
Pueblo Revolt of 1680 49, 54, 157
Puente de Piedra 87
Pugh Ranch 127
Putnam 53
Pyote 144

Q

Quantrill, William C. 18, 95, 103, 162
Quest Geo-Marine 146
Quick Killer (Tats-ah-das-ay-go) 69
Quintana 20
Quitman Mountains 154

R

Rabb's Creek 84
Rader Ridge 48
Ramirez Creek 87
Ramon (ferryman) 32
Ramsdale's Crossing and Ferry 121
Rancho de los Olmos 82
Rancho Santa Cruz 41
Rattler Community 103
Reagan brothers 27
Reagan, Frank 26
Reagan, Jim 26
Reagan, John 26
Reagan, Lee 26
Realitos 53
Red Hill 51
Red River 45, 57, 60, 61, 105, 150,
     156, 158
Refugio 120
Reine de Mers (*Reine de Mars*) (French ship) 37
Richards, Billy 108
Riddle, William 131
Rincon del Oso 122
Rio Grande 22, 23, 26, 32, 35, 52,
     54, 56, 69, 83, 94, 95, 108, 114,

115, 127, 141, 142, 145, 150,
     151, 157, 159, 161, 166
Rio Grande City 127
Rio Priato 48
Riverside Ranch 108
Robbers Roost 102
Robert (man) 67
Robinson 55
Robstown 110
Rock Creek 121
Rockport 10
Rodriguez, Montez Veronica 141
Roma 127
Rose family 143
Rosillos Mountain 23
Rosston 45
Round Mountain 51, 134
Roundout, Illinois 18
Round Rock 128, 133, 147, 148, 163
Routh, H.C. 149
Routh, Mary Elizabeth 149
Runaway Scrape 160
Rustler Hills 49
Rustler Spring 49
Rutherford, Philip R. 81

S

Sabinal 139
Sabinal River 139, 140
Sabine Pass 75
Sabine River 70, 121
Sabine (ship) 60
Sacramento Mountains 32
Salado 14, 15
Salado Creek 15, 19
Salt Creek 112
Samuels 144
San Angelo 133, 138
San Antone 48
San Antonio 12, 13, 16, 18, 19, 24, 27,
     52, 69, 77, 83, 89, 97, 98, 100,
     107, 114, 124, 135, 141, 155,
     157, 158, 160

San Antonio Crossing 82
San Antonio River 76
San Augustine 122
San Bernard River 20
San Cajo Mountain 97
San Cajo Mountains 98
Sanderson 25
Sand Point 30
Sandy Creek 91
San Estevan (Spanish ship) 146, 153
San Francisco River 22
San Gabriel River 102, 148
San Jacinto 63, 82, 117, 143, 145
San Luis Pass 59
San Marcos 93
San Patricio 109, 123
San Pedro (Spanish ship) 37
San Saba (city) 124
San Saba mines 12
San Saba Presidio 12, 13, 88, 100, 101,
    155, 157, 158
San Saba River 99, 100, 101, 102,
    123, 124, 125, 155, 157
Santa Anna, General Antonio Lopez
    de 16, 29, 30, 52, 63, 64, 72,
    82, 97, 109, 117, 134, 143, 145,
    160, 161
Santa Anna Mountain 44
Santa Anna Mountains 44
Santa Fe, New Mexico 77, 106, 119
Santa Maria de Guadalupe (Spanish ship)
    42
Santa Maria de Yciar (Spanish ship) 147,
    153
Santa Rita 35, 159
Santa Rosa (Spanish ship) 31, 120
Santiago Mountains 26
Santiago (sheepherder) 142
San Ygnacio 151
Schnault Springs 50
Seabrook 63
Seminole Hill 18, 141, 142
Sems Ranch 32
Seven Rocks Hill 98

1766 hurricane 58
Shackelford, R. E., 15
Shafter 114, 115, 154
Shafter Lake 9
Shafter, William "Pecos Bill" 9
Shamrock Island 110
Shaner, Florence E. (author) 138
Sheffield 113
Shelton Hollow 65
Shephard, Clell 113, 138
Shephard, Oliver 113, 138
Shiner Ranch 98
Shipp Ranch 145
Shoal Creek 134
Sierra de las Cenizas (Mountain of the
    Ashes) 49
Sierra Diablo Mountains 47
Sierra Nevada Mountains 142
Signal Mountain 68
Silver Cloud (ship) 64
Silver Creek 90, 100, 101
Silver Mine Creek 154
Singer, Alexander 41
Singer, Isaac 41
Singer, John 41
Singer Ranch 41
Sivell's Bend 105
S. J. Lee (ship) 37
Skeen's Peak 112
Smugglers Trail 22
Snively 102
Snively, Major Jacob 142
Southern Pacific Railroad 24, 25, 144
South Llano River 88
Spanish-American War 9, 133
Spanish Camp 145
Spanish Fort 104, 105, 142, 158
Spanish Trail 66, 85, 106, 136, 141
Spofford 79
Springtown 112
Spy Knob 71
Stanton 92
Steinheimer, Karl 15
Sterling City 128

Stewart, Henry 137
Stillhouse Hollow Reservoir 15
St. Joseph, Missouri 163
St. Joseph (San Jose) Island 10, 11, 42
St. Louis, Missouri 15, 57, 66, 106, 121, 124
St. Marys 120
Stockton 132
Stogden, Frank 48
Sublett, Ben (Will or William) 49
Sublett, Ross 49
Sudduth 28
Sue Peak 25
Sugar Loaf Mound 141
Sugar Loaf Mountain 141
Sulphur Springs 67
Sweeney, Hap 47
Sweetwater 107
Synder, Captain 19

T

Tabira (Gran Quivira), New Mexico 48
Tarzan 92
Tascosa 111, 117
Tatum 120, 121
Tatum, Fox 121
Taylor, General Zachary 32, 36
Tecolote Mountains 119
Temple 14, 15
Terlingua 21, 22
Terrazas, Luiz 23
Terry, Thomas P. (author) 8
Texas Antiquities Committee 147
Texas Attorney General 146
Texas Land Commissioners Office 146
Texas Pacific 92
Texas Rangers 18, 25, 46, 52, 60, 71, 88, 91, 103, 114, 140, 150, 163
Texas State Marine Archeologist 166
Thicket 114
Thorndale 102
Threadgill Creek 93

Three Mile Hill 110
Three Rivers 87, 88
Tierra Draw 111
Tiger Lake 30
Tigertown 81
Tigre Ranch 14
Tonkawas 12, 96, 157
Tontino (person) 110
Tornillo River 23
Tower Hill 128
Toyahvale (Toyah) 118
Trammel, Gaspar (Caspar) 120
Trammel Trail 120
Trans-Pecos 154
Treaties of Velasco 161
Treaty of Guadalupe-Hidalgo 161
Trinity 135
Trinity Bay 63
Trinity River 50, 64, 86, 91, 107, 135, 156
Tripett, Frank (author) 162
Trout Bayou 121
Tubbs, William 96
Turgen Gang 53
Turkey Creek 140, 151

U

Union Pacific Railroad 51
Urrea, General Jose de 160
Uvalde 140

V

Vaca, Cabeza de 166
Valentine 73
Van Horn 47, 74, 154
Vanlisten, Frank 84
Vargas, Diego de 157
Vasquez, Delores Agilero 16, 79, 110, 127, 159
Veatch, Mark 72
Veracruz, Mexico 11, 39, 138, 152, 153
Victoria 143

Villa, Pancho 16, 17, 55, 56, 79, 110,
        127, 159
Villareal, Captain Enrique 122
Vincente Canyon 22
Vincent's Point 11
Virginia Point 58

W

Waco 66, 96
Wallisville 43
Wall, Tom 118
Walnut Bend 45, 105
Walters, Dr. Bradford 138
War of Texas Independence 84, 119, 160
Washington, Hans 59
Wayne, Wailing 39
Weatherford 112
Wedig, John 30
West Fork of the Trinity River 11
West Mountain 131
White, Joe 107
White's Point 122
White (veteran) 84
Wichita Falls 11
Wildcat Crossing 107
Wilkinson Ranch 99
Wilkinson's Hole 99
Wilkinson, W.J. "Jack" 99
Williams, Sam 103
Wilson, Mike 49
Wilson, Steve (author) 104, 129
Wimberly 65
Wise Creek 149
Wolf Creek 107
Woods, Dee (author) 109, 138
Wooten, Dr. Joseph S. 94
Wooton, Bill 137
Wyman, John 151

Y

Yacht (ship) 39
Yellowstone (ship) 21

Z

Zieglar, Jacob 110
Znika brothers 153

ABOUT THE AUTHOR

W. Craig Gaines is the author of *Hispanic Treasure of the Eastern United States*; *Hispanic Treasures of the Western United States*; *The Confederate Cherokees: John Drew's Regiment of Mounted Rifles*; *Encyclopedia of Civil War Shipwrecks*; *Civil War Gold and Other Lost Treasures*; *California Treasure and Treasure Tales*; *Great Lost Treasure Never Found*; *Lost Oklahoma Treasure* and other books and articles. Craig has been interested in lost treasure since seeing the film *Treasure Island* when he was very young. He has written lost treasure stories for a variety of treasure-hunting magazines over the years. Craig is an engineer, geologist and writer who has visited many of the areas mentioned in this work. He and his wife, Arla, live in Tulsa, Oklahoma.

Opposite: Craig as a five-year-old cowboy. *Author.*

Visit us at
www.historypress.com
....